Creative Development

Florence Beetlestone

Activities based on the Desirable Outcomes for under-fives

Ideas for planning, assessment and record-keeping

Photocopiable stories, rhymes and songs

Author
Florence Beetlestone

Series consultant
Pauline Kenyon

Editor
Sally Gray

Assistant editor
Lesley Sudlow

Series designer
Joy White

Designer
Rachel Warner

Illustrations
Roma Bishop

Cover and photographs
Garry Clarke

Designed using Adobe Pagemaker
Processed by Scholastic Ltd, Leamington Spa

Published by Scholastic Ltd, Villiers House, Clarendon Avenue,
Leamington Spa, Warwickshire CV32 5PR

© 1998 Scholastic Ltd   Text © 1998 Florence Beetlestone
234567890   8901234567

With thanks to Military Road Lower School in Northampton and Rainbows End Nursery in Leamington Spa for allowing us to photograph their work with the children.

The publishers gratefully acknowledge permission to reproduce the following copyright material: **Sue Cowling** for 'Give A Hat, Take A Hat' © 1998 Sue Cowling, previously unpublished. **Jillian Harker** for 'The New Kite' and 'Taki's Picnic' © 1998 Jillian Harker, previously unpublished. **Her Majesty's Stationery Office** for the use of text from the Department of Education and Employment/SCAA document *Nursery Education Desirable Outcomes for Children's Learning* © 1996, Crown copyright. **Jan Holdstock** for 'Every Colour Under The Sun' from *Every Colour Under The Sun* by Jan Holdstock © 1983 Jan Holdstock (1983, Ward Lock Educational). **Johanne Levy** for 'Mixing Colours' and 'Rainbow Song' © 1998 Johanne Levy, previously unpublished. **Tony Mitton** for 'Pattern Making', 'Going On Holiday' and 'Painting' © 1998 Tony Mitton and 'I Am' from *More Acorns* © 1995 Tony Mitton (1995, OUP, Oxford Reading Tree). **Judith Nicholls** for 'Animal Chatter' and 'Can You Hear?' © 1998 Judith Nicholls, previously unpublished. Every effort has been made to trace copyright holders and the publishers apologise for any inadvertent omissions.

British Library Cataloguing-in-Publication Data
A catalogue record for this book is available from the British Library.

ISBN 0-590-53761-X

Contents

Introduction – page 5

Chapter one: Planning – page 9

Chapter two: Child development – page 15

Chapter three: Assessment and record-keeping – page 19

Chapter four: Music – page 23
A rainy day – page 23
Sing a song of sixpence – page 24
All clap hands – page 25
Tap that rhythm – page 26
Musical moments – page 27
Bells and jingles – page 28
Shaker fun – page 29
Fun with sounds – page 30
The music shop – page 31
Doh, ray, me... – page 32

Chapter five: Art – page 33
Black and white – page 33
Simple printing blocks – page 34
Oranges and lemons – page 35
Exploring seeds – page 36
Colourful crayons – page 37
Blot painting – page 38
Straw patterns – page 39
Marbling fun – page 40
Our art gallery – page 41
Flour paste patterns – page 42

Chapter six: Craft – page 43
Unbreakable plates – page 43
Moulding materials – page 44
Make a book – page 45
Fun with junk – page 46
Receding shapes – page 47
Tiling patterns – page 48
Fruit feast – page 49
The mad hatter – page 50
Cards for all occasions – page 51
Dress a puppet – page 52

Chapter seven: Dance and drama – page 53

Let's act it out – page 53
Guess the rhyme – page 54
Puppet fun – page 55
Tell-a-story figures – page 56
My journey to nursery – page 57
Ring-o-ring-o-roses – page 58
Take your partners – page 59
A windy day – page 60
Animal antics – page 61
A walk in the woods – page 62

Chapter eight: Imaginative play – page 63

Going on a picnic – page 63
Sunshine tours – page 64
Fire station – page 65
Snip 'n' style – page 66
Nine to five – page 67
Mary, Mary... – page 68
Bases for play – page 69
Kitchen furniture – page 70
Take a hat and a bag... – page 71
What could this be? – page 72

Photocopiable assessment and record-keeping sheets – page 73

Music – page 73
Art and craft – page 74
Dance and drama – page 75
Imaginative play – page 76

Photocopiable rhymes, stories and songs – page 77

RHYMES – Pattern making – page 77
Going on holiday – 78
Painting – page 79
Can you hear? – 80
Animal chatter – page 80
Give a hat, take a hat – page 81
I am – page 82
STORIES – The new kite – page 83
Taki's picnic – page 84
SONGS – Mixing colours – page 85
Rainbow song – page 86
Every colour under the sun – page 87

Photocopiable activity sheets – page 88

Listen carefully – page 88
Bang the drums – page 89
Symmetry – page 90
Junk modelling props – page 91
Fun with hats – page 92
Animal puppets – page 93
Three little pigs – page 94
Signs to use – page 95

Recommended resources – page 96

Introduction

Young children's creative development involves them in fascinating explorations of sound, materials, colours and textures using all their senses. It is an area in which they are encouraged to use their imaginations to the full and express their developing ideas and feelings.

This book shows how you can provide planned opportunities for children's creative development following the guidelines set down in *Nursery Education: Desirable Outcomes for children's learning on entering compulsory education*, published by the School Curriculum and Assessment Authority for use in England. The ideas in this book can also be applied equally well to the guidance documents on pre-school education published for Wales, Scotland and Northern Ireland.

The Desirable Outcomes

The Desirable Outcomes for Creative Development state that:

Children explore sound and colour, texture, shape, form and space in two and three dimensions. They respond in a variety of ways to what they see, hear, smell, touch and feel. Through art, music, dance, stories and imaginative play, they show an increasing ability to use their imagination, to listen and to observe. They use a widening range of materials, suitable tools, instruments and other resources to express ideas and to communicate their feelings.

All these areas are carefully addressed in the five activity chapters in this book, which are divided in the following way:
* Chapter 4: Music;
* Chapter 5: Art;
* Chapter 6: Craft;
* Chapter 7: Drama and dance;
* Chapter 8: Imaginative play.

Useful information on the range of resources that you might collect to support creative learning is given on page 96.

Planning

Creative Development should be planned alongside each of the other five Areas of Learning, as in many cases it overlaps and reinforces learning across the curriculum. Look for ways in which creativity can be developed in other curriculum areas, for example by choosing science activities that will foster a greater understanding of texture. Look at the creative potential of all equipment, such as jigsaws and construction toys and of routine tasks such as hanging up coats.

Whatever your setting, make sure that you maximise the potential of the activities you are following and the equipment you have. Creative activities can often be enhanced very simply by using inexpensive junk materials.

Your planning needs to cover the long-term (a year, or two-year rolling programme), medium-term (a term or half-term) and the short-term (weekly and daily planning in more detail). More information on this is supplied in Chapter 1 – Planning.

Equal opportunities

All activities need to be planned to ensure that all children can take part and benefit equally. Consider any special needs which your children may have and adapt activities, resources and your approach accordingly. Ensure that girls and boys are not limited in their opportunities by gender stereotypical resources or teaching approach.

Plan activities that create opportunities for new experiences and include in your planning an appreciation of the experience that the children bring with them. For example, use the children's experiences of holidays abroad as the basis of role-play, or use tapes of music heard at home. Ensure that children can experience a variety of cultural traditions in music, dance, art, craft and imaginative play. Check that your resources, particularly books, pictures and artefacts reflect this wider world.

Involving artists, musicians and craftspeople

Children enjoy looking at the ways in which other people have painted, modelled or made music. Keep sets of postcards, photographs and books so that children can look at the work of other artists. If you are following a theme of 'fruit' then you can collect some examples of artist's drawings and paintings of fruit – there are a large number of still life examples to choose from. Similarly you can provide examples of music which fit particular themes. Children like to hear about people and if you tell some simple stories about artists it will capture their imagination. Make sure that you always provide a range of examples from different cultures and provide examples of women as well as men. Keep your discussions simple, but encourage children to begin to look critically at art and listen critically to music by discussing what they like/dislike about examples and why.

Keep audio and visual extracts short; long enough to give children a flavour of the mood and style, yet not so long that they become restless. Five to ten minutes is enough time for listening activities. If the activity also involves watching or participating in some way then ten to fifteen minutes will be suitable.

Safety

Key reminders about safety are noted on the relevant activity pages. Always think about safety aspects when setting up and organising activities. Statutory requirements regarding health and safety will need to be followed for all movement activities. For example, all equipment which might be used for imaginative play, such as a climbing frame or beams and tunnels must be in good order and surrounded by soft mats. Such activities should always be supervised by at least one adult, and numbers of children undertaking large scale physical activities should be limited by the amount of personal space available to each child. Think about the safety of children dancing, skipping and jumping when many children will be moving about vigorously in small spaces. Similarly, safety regulations cover the use of certain tools, such as saws, screwdrivers or knives which may be used in craft activities. Keep all sharp tools out of reach of children when not in use.

When taking the children on an outing, check the Local Authority regulations for the correct adult to child ratio. Send a letter home to parents/carers asking for their permission to take their child on outings. Make sure that you are aware of any allergies, illnesses or other health considerations concerning the children.

Display

Displays can be two-dimensional or three-dimensional and arranged on walls, hung from ceilings or set out on table tops. Try to have a mixture of displays so that the eye is taken not only to the edges of the room but to the floor and ceiling too. Shoe boxes draped with fabric can create height/shelves/different levels on table-top displays. Fabric can also be draped behind as a background.

Where possible displays should enable children to interact with them – include items to handle, labels and books, pose questions to be answered and problems to be solved. For example a colour table might include some pieces of coloured acetate with the question: What colours do you see when you look through? Wall displays can have pockets or flaps which encourage children to look closely, rather like the open-up flaps in books. Add questions to the displays, such as: How many shapes can you see? Mount collages and small models using white glue which is strong enough to hold even quite heavy objects. Other larger models and buildings can be displayed on tables or on floor mats like exhibits at an art exhibition. Photographs can be displayed in albums or in books you have made with the children.

Displays should be used as a learning resource, and children should be involved in setting them up. In this way they can make decisions about how things look and begin to develop aesthetic judgements. Displays should always look attractive and be mounted to enhance the children's work. Using neutral colour background mounts or tonal contrast – light on dark or dark on light – sets off work well. A black line drawn round the edge 'frames' pictures, and when mounting several pictures together mount them in an imaginary frame so that the eye is drawn to an overall shape. Displays can also be linked together by themes, for example a theme of pattern could unify sets of models, paintings, drawings, fabric work and photographs of children engaged in making movement patterns.

Captions written by an adult should be well spaced, neat and legible, presenting a good model. Use a mix of upper and lower case letters in the normal way.

If you are unable to set up permanent displays you can make charts and display areas very simply by making hangings from wallpaper or fabric. These can be put up and taken down very quickly and rolled up at the end of sessions. Keep collections of display items in boxes that can easily be brought out and set up on display tables.

Assessment and record-keeping

Carefully planned assessment and record-keeping is crucial, both for understanding what the children can achieve now and for addressing their needs for the future. Knowledge about the way in which young children develop is essential to inform assessment and this is outlined in Chapter 2 – Child development. Detailed guidance on all aspects of assessment and record-keeping is given in Chapter 3 – Assessment and record-keeping. There are also photocopiable assessment and recording sheets on pages 73–76 to help you keep a record of assessment in all areas of creative learning.

Working with parents

Throughout the book there is an understanding that parents are an integral part of their children's education and ideas for sharing the learning programme are indicated in each activity. Ensure that all your planning and record-keeping is shared with parents. Show them how you intend to cover Creative Development. Make a book of photographs to use with parents, showing some of the typical activities that may be undertaken, such as a music and movement session, children singing and acting out nursery rhymes and clay work.

How to use this book

This book sets out how to plan an effective Creative Development curriculum within your group. The initial chapters show you how to plan, taking into account children's stages of development, and how to assess and record the learning that is taking place. The activity chapters focus on music, art, craft, drama and dance and imaginative play and on pages 88–95 you will find photocopiable activities to reinforce and extend the learning.

The book also contains a specially compiled selection of stories, rhymes and songs. Ideas on how they can be used are given in the activities.

Other books in this series

There are seven books in the *Learning in the Early Years* series. Six of the books each cover one of the Areas of Learning in the Desirable Outcomes listed by SCAA. These are:
* *Mathematics.*
* *Language and Literacy.*
* *Personal and Social Development.*
* *Knowledge and Understanding of the World.*
* *Creative Development.*
* *Physical Development.*

The seventh book in the series, *Ready for Inspection*, provides practical guidance on all the management issues that groups will need to tackle in order to deliver the outcomes effectively and efficiently, and prepare for a successful inspection.

chapter one

Planning

Planning is an essential ingredient for providing quality early years' provision. By thorough and careful planning you will ensure that you are presenting children with a balanced programme that meets both the needs of the children and the requirements of the Desirable Outcomes.

The importance of planning

Many adults are very good organisers and able to plan well-balanced sessions in their heads. They may also be very good at deciding how they will manage other adults and children, by thinking through their ideas and discussing them on an informal basis. This does however leave a lot to chance – some things may get left out and coverage of certain areas may be poor. In order to plan effectively and thoroughly to take in considerations such as coverage of all Areas of Learning, provision for special needs children, opportunities to explore a broad range of themes and activities and activities that plan for the progression of the children's skills and abilities, it is essential to implement a rigorous and systematic planning procedure for your group. Therefore, it is now required that plans are written and that they clearly identify how the learning outcomes are to be covered.

Preparing for inspection

When your group is inspected your provision for Creative Development will be evaluated against the following criteria.

Are the children given opportunities to:

* explore sound?
* explore colour, texture, shape, space and form in two- and three- dimensions?
* respond in a variety of ways to what they see, hear, smell, touch and feel?
* show increasing ability to listen, observe, and use imagination through art, music, dance, stories and imaginative play?
* use a widening range of materials, suitable tools, musical instruments and other resources to express ideas and to communicate feelings?

They will expect to see children engaged in activities which promote these aspects and will also expect to see that these have been planned for and that the plans are linked to the way in which progress in these aspects is recorded.

The Creative Development curriculum

It is helpful, when planning, to divide up Creative Development into five sub-areas. The activity chapters in this book each represent one of these sub-areas. They are: Music, Art, Craft, Dance and drama and Imaginative play. By covering these areas of the curriculum we are helping to ensure that we are promoting the child's musical, artistic, imaginative and physical development, all of which are needed if a child is to be creative. If they are planned for separately you can ensure that you are giving a good balanced programme for Creative Development and that the outcomes identified above will all be met. As these areas are all very closely linked they can be taught very effectively through themes. When planning thematically it is still important to ensure balanced coverage, but in this case you may wish to use the sub-areas more as reminders rather than headings.

The planning cycle

Ensure that all planning is done together as a staff team so that everyone is clear about the learning involved. You will find it helpful to plan for the long-, medium-, and short-term.

Long-term planning

Depending on the number of sessions that you are running, and how long children are in your setting, you may decide to cover all of the learning outcomes identified under Creative Development over one or two years. If children generally stay for more than one year in your setting you may wish to devise a two-year rolling programme to avoid direct repetition of skills and topics.

Your long-term plans will need to identify the learning outcomes for the year in respect of all the six Areas of Learning. You may decide to plan your work in themes, and your long-term plans will then identify the way you will meet the learning outcomes under these themes for each term or half-term (see below).

For Creative Development you will need to indicate in your long-term plans how you intend to cover the outcomes for this area. Use the sub-headings of art, music and so on to help you do this. Each term you will identify your particular focus. For example, you may decide to focus on 'exploring sound' in the spring term with a number of musical activities. Ensure that music, art, dance and drama and imaginative play are, however, all experienced each term. Avoid long gaps between the types of activity, as this will limit the children's potential to grow in these skill areas.

Creative Development	*Assessment opportunities	LONG-TERM PLANNING
	Topics/focus	Comments
A u t u m n (term)	Autumn (6 weeks) Art – leaf printing* Craft – making moulds Music – songs about autumn* Imaginative play – home corner –'wood' Dance/drama – 'Walk in the woods'	Display of autumn leaves, fruits and berries Go on autumn walk Vivaldi's *Four Seasons*, 'Autumn'
	Light and colour (6 weeks) Art – use a range of paint colours, colour mixing* Craft – make candle holders and divas Music – poems, songs about colour and light, 'light and dark' sounds Imaginative play – set up decorators shop in home corner* Dance/drama – act out festival of light, dance colours*	Set up colour table display Link to range of festivals; Divali and Christmas Play mood tapes about night
S p r i n g (term)	Baby Animals (5 weeks) Art – draw/paint animals* Craft – collage animals/junk models Music – listen to animal sounds, make these with instruments Imaginative play – Pet shop Dance/drama – animal movements/going to the zoo*	Make simple masks/tunics for role-play of baby animals Zoo/farm or pet shop visit
	Trees (6 weeks) Art – bark rubbings Craft – make moulds of cones and bark Music – make tree name rhythms, listen to music* Imaginative play – provide props for role-play about tree cutting Dance/drama – act out tree movements	Play a tape of *Pastoral Symphony*
S u m m e r (term)	Holidays (6 weeks) Art – postcard collage Craft – making passports* Music – cultural music Imaginative play – Travel agents Dance/drama – 'Going on a picnic', story and drama	Set up picnic props for imaginative play after story Selection of tapes of traditional music, such as Flamenco/Spain
	Weather (7 weeks) Art – paint weather pictures Craft – make papier mâché/card 'suns' Music – instruments to create weather sounds, weather songs* Imaginative play – wet weather shop Dance/drama – 'Going on holiday' movement*	Display of cards featuring pictures of weather Set up props: macs/boots/umbrellas Set up props for sunny weather/suitcases

Medium-term planning

Medium-term plans should indicate your planning for each half-term or term. For Creative Development indicate how you are planning each of the five sub-areas and the sorts of activities which will be used to meet the learning outcomes. For example, if you have identified 'exploring sound' as your focus, you may outline under 'music' such activities as 'making shakers with a variety of objects' or 'making a tape of sounds heard in the nursery'. You may well find it helpful to set out medium-term plans in linear format reflecting a weekly spread of activities (see the example, below).

Creative Development	*Assessment opportunities — MEDIUM-TERM PLANNING
Topics/focus	**Comments**
Week 1 Autumn Leaf printing using autumn colours* Make leaf moulds using clay and different leaf shapes Song – 'One conker, Two conkers...' (to 'One potato' tune) Make trees from paper and junk 'A walk in the woods' (dance)	Talk about autumn leaves, changing colours Go for a walk in the woods. Record the sounds made by rustling leaves.
Week 2 Sort leaves into different shapes Use leaf moulds for display Listen to Vivaldi's *Four Seasons* 'A walk in the woods' (dance)	Make a collage of leaves and seeds/fruits Encourage children to describe how it feels in the woods
Week 3 Print with leaves Photograph the leaves before and after the moulds for display Autumn songs Paint giant trees for the home corner 'A walk in the woods' (dance session)	Listen to rustling leaves again Develop vocabulry to describe walking and 'the woods' Use small world trees and a play board to set up the 'woods' Read stories such as 'The three bears' and 'Little Red Riding Hood'

Short-term planning

Short-term plans will identify what is to be covered each week more precisely and daily plans will show which activities are to be set up and where. For example: Blue group and Margaret – craft table, 'Making pastry' 9.30 –11.30. Daily plans can take various formats: as timetables; lists of activities; on pre-designed sheets; in note form or on diagrammatic plans (see below for an example).

Creative Development	Autumn Term/Weekly grid			SHORT-TERM PLANNING	
	Monday	**Tuesday**	**Wednesday**	**Thursday**	**Friday**
Art/Craft 9.00–11.00	Painting with easels using green/yellow/ brown and orange paints (Mary)	Sort leaf shapes children have brought in. Feel textures, talk about shapes. Show how mould is made (Ann)	Use autumn colours with orange and green paper (Mary)		
Music 11.30		←———	Whole group singing conker song All listen to a piece from Vivaldi just before story (Jane)	——→	Play again at milk time
Imaginative play 10.15–11.30	All week ——→ Paint trees onto large sheets of paper to decorate home corner screens. Make background frieze about walk in the woods. Discuss how children feel about woods. Small world play with trees and base board. (Jane to set up and organise)				
Dance/drama					Prepare for Autumn walk next Tuesday. Discuss what we may find (Ann)

Balance, continuity and progression

Long-term planning enables you to get an overall picture of the work you intend children to follow for the year. As you look at this picture you will be able to check that activities follow on and that skills are gradually developed. Ensure that you look at plans for the previous year, and where children are in your setting for longer than a year, you will need to plan your programme so that skills and knowledge are built up progressively over this full period. Using the guidelines for Creative Development in Chapter 2, page 15, ensure that skills and knowledge are promoted systematically over each term so that progress is assured. For example, in the first weeks you may wish to teach children how to handle brushes and pencils, and in the next few weeks to provide activities which enable them to use brushes and pencils in a variety of ways.

Assessment and record-keeping

Use the notes that you make about the way children perform in an activity to inform your planning. When you devise your weekly and daily plans use these ongoing assessments to make minor adjustments to long-term plans. For example, when creating your yearly plan you may have allocated only a few sessions to learning how to handle musical instruments, but in practice you find that you need to extend these activities for another half-term.

Whenever you review the children's assessment folders, look carefully not just at individual progress but about what needs to be developed. These needs can then form the basis of individual development plans which can be built in to medium- and short-term planning. For example, when checking the records it may be obvious that most of the children need more experience of working with clay in which case the plans for the next half-term can be adjusted. In other cases individual needs may be identified. For example, a child may be using their imagination to make up stories when playing with the dolls' house and you may wish to develop this skill further through an activity such as puppet play when planning your weekly and daily plans. Further guidance on assessment and record-keeping is given in Chapter 3.

Planning considerations

Using questions

Much of your communication with children will be through asking questions, but do however try to achieve a balance. Ask open-ended questions and encourage the children to ask their own, allowing them time to put their thoughts into words. For each activity there is a list of suggested questions to help the children to focus on the task. Use these as a guideline, but be prepared to follow up on the children's interests and ideas. Ensure that the children have opportunities to talk to you and each other while they are engaged in the task. Then use

your questions to gently prompt a child, focus their attention or to develop their ideas further.

Children's questions and comments are very revealing. Have a notebook and pen handy to jot down some of these comments to form the basis of records later (see Chapter 3).

Organising activities

Try to plan an equal mix of activities each day; some that are teacher-intensive and some that allow the children to express their own ideas and initiate their own play (such as easel painting, free play with dough, dressing-up, small world play and mats for jumping, hopping or lying on). It is important however that all planned activities have a clear learning objective, such as experimenting with a new media or consolidating colour mixing.

Try to create a balance in the way that you set up equipment and activities. Construction toys for example may sometimes be used for free play where children explore the colour, shapes and textures of the bricks and may sometimes form the basis of an adult-directed activity, for example, making patterns using different coloured bricks. Similarly an activity like marbling should not always be adult-directed. Children will benefit from having some time to randomly experiment with mixing the colours of the marbling inks in their own way. All activities benefit from adult direction at some time and will also need to be used freely. Consider using them like this:

free play – children explore
↓
directed – teach skill
↓
free play – further exploration of skill
↓
direction – extend the skill
↓
free play – consolidate and apply skills
↓
direction – teach new skills

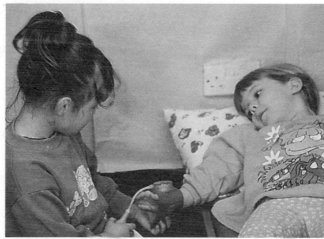

Equal opportunities

Each child is entitled to receive the same curriculum and no child should be disadvantaged by gender, race, religion or class. You will need to be alert to the times when restrictions or limitations may occur. For example, if you are planning a hospital corner, arrange ways in which both boys and girls can take on all the roles. Children often quite naturally do this, but sometimes may be inhibited by the comments of other children. Make sure that the range of resources you are using encourages boys and girls to take up a variety of roles. Arrange time for adults to join in imaginative play so that they can discuss roles and extend the children's ideas.

When planning, think carefully about the resources you are going to use – the books, pictures, videos, artefacts and equipment. Plan outside visits and invite visitors in to broaden experiences. Ensure that these resources reflect diversity, encouraging 'sensitivity to others, including those of different cultures and beliefs'. Think about the range of art, music and design to be found in different countries and some of the different styles, techniques and approaches you can use to reflect this. The activities in this book include ideas which will help you to do this effectively.

Draw upon the experiences of the children in your group and discuss any community events whenever possible. Festivals, such as the celebration of Eid or the Chinese New Year can provide a focus for creative work and you should consider this when planning.

Teamwork and support

You will be working as part of a staff team. Each member of the team will need to be clear about their role – who is doing what? In particular, who is ensuring that there are correct resources, setting up and working with each activity. Who will be assessing and when? How do you wish records to be made? You may wish all staff to have experience in all areas and organise them on a rota basis. Or you may wish to assign Creative Development to one person who has a particular interest/ expertise in this area giving them responsibility. Your short-term plans should indicate this clearly (see previous example).

Similarly parent helpers need to be clear about expectations when they are in your setting. How often are they expected to help? Which table(s) will they be working on? For how long? With which children? Are they expected to help with clearing away, washing-up or milk time? It is useful to write down simple guidelines for parents which can be used each time.

When planning, identify which activities require extra adult help, such as going on a walk or cooking and where you wish parents to work on a daily basis. Make notes about any particular items you wish parents to bring in or any skills which you may wish to check with them.

Your plans will also need to indicate what is expected of the children. How will the children choose activities? Will they choose all of the time or occasionally? How is the balance of the day worked out? (Free play, directed time, milk, coats, story, introduction to the session, carpet time and so on.) How are you going to organise these periods and how will you manage the change-overs between them? Your planning will need to identify which time you are allocating for whole class work, which for groups and which for individual work. Devise a simple format, but keep it clear.

Evaluation

All plans will need to be evaluated regularly, and you will want to adjust the way you write and present plans as a result of working with different formats. Build in a system where you can do this, for example holding short meetings at the end of each week to discuss any key points, and longer meetings at the end of each half-term with all the staff involved. It is also useful for individuals to have regular times to discuss their views on a one-to-one basis with the leader/manager.

The planning checklist below can be used as a quick reminder:
* Have you included Creative Development as one of your six Areas of Learning?
* Have you indicated how you will develop art, craft, music, dance, drama and imaginative play?
* Do your plans show how the learning outcomes will be met?
* Do your plans build on previous plans and do children build on their prior learning?
* Are your plans linked to your assessments?
* Do they show a good balance between adult-directed and child-initiated activities?
* Have you identified what resources are needed, including visits/visitors?
* Do your plans clearly indicate how you are ensuring equal opportunities?
* Is your daily timetable clear, showing your normal routine?
* Do your plans show what is expected of staff, parents and children?
* Have you built in a procedure for checking and evaluating plans?

chapter two

Child development

It is most important when selecting and introducing activities for creative development that these are appropriate for this age group. In order to do this it is helpful to have an idea of the stages of development which are typical of this age span. This chapter provides you with some useful background information.

Creative activities will often contain skills which overlap curriculum areas, for example in plucking the rubber band strings of a home-made guitar, the child is learning not just about musical sound, but is also developing the fine motor skills which aid physical development.

All development at this age is characterised by the child's need to explore both materials and the environment and to discover how he or she interacts with it. For example, children need to find out that dry sand has a grainy texture and can slip easily through the fingers, and that wet sand can feel quite smooth when covered with a thin film of water and can also be moulded into shapes.

Artistic development

Four stages of development have been identified in respect of children's drawings – The Scribbling stage, Pre-schematic stage, Schematic stage and Visual realism. These are generally used as the model for analysing levels of artistic development and they provide us with useful guidelines. Children between the ages of three and five will fall under the first two categories.

* *Scribbling stage* – (up to about four/ five years) – the child is busy exploring her environment through her senses. She expresses these through random markings, exploration of colour, space and three-dimensional materials. These marks gradually become more continuous and controlled.

* *Pre-schematic* – (about four to six years) – the child expresses real or imagined experiences with her first attempts at representation.

Developing artistic skills

Activities will centre around the use of paint, graphic materials and collage.

Painting should include opportunities to mix colours, gradually leading to an awareness of the importance of primary colours and to the way in which colours can be lightened by adding white. Activities will include painting and printing using a variety of techniques and tools.

Graphic activities will include drawing with pencils, pens, inks, charcoal and crayons. Children should be encouraged to work freely so that they develop their understanding of lines (both straight and curved) and the way that marks can be placed within a given space.

Collage work allows children to think about shapes, textures and patterns.

Developing craft skills

This covers activities which involve more than two-dimensional work and include the making of artefacts, buildings or models and sculpture, which all involve ways of using three-dimensional materials in an artistic way. Sculpture can involve different methods of dealing with materials to create new objects:

* materials which can be shaped – clay, plaster, dough, snow, mud, sand and Plasticine (these provide a sensual, manipulative experience);
* reclaimed materials which can be put together by tying, gluing, slotting or folding – boxes, cartons, tins, wire (bent or shaped), wood (cut and joined);
* carving – soap, plaster, polystyrene, hard clay, wood, stone;
* fabrics stuffed, sewn, stapled or glued into three-dimensional forms;
* metals or resins that can be cast in moulds.

A child's first experience of three-dimensional art usually comes through using building blocks, which can be seen as a form of sculpture. Modelling or sculpting provides a way for young children to learn about shape and form of solid objects. Handling clay has a particular importance to a child's aesthetic development, because the child learns to have mastery over the material in a way that is not possible with other materials.

Musical development

Children between the ages of three and five years are beginning to differentiate between objects and can start to understand that musical instruments have a purpose which is different from that of a toy. Musical instruments can be introduced as part of a singing and music session where children can begin to explore the potential of musical instruments as tools. At this age children love experimenting with new words and sounds and should be able to concentrate for 20–30 minutes every day, participating in a music and singing session. Through music they will also develop socially by taking turns, learning to listen and building relationships through working together. In addition they will experience a sense of achievement, gain positive feelings of acceptance and belonging and develop respect for all cultures through singing and music from various cultures.

They will gradually be learning about composing and inventing by exploring how sounds can be organised into a means of individual expression. In singing and playing they will be recreating musical ideas and developing their understanding of time and rhythm. For example, they will begin to recognise that rhythms are the same or different, and can be at different speeds through making their own musical sequences and in clapping simple rhythms such as their names. They will also be becoming increasingly aware of pitch – particularly of high and low sounds. The deepening of listening skills is very important at this age. As children focus their attention on the music they will be developing their aural memory and will become more adept at sound recognition and discrimination.

Activities to develop musical skills

Regular activities which should be followed include:
* singing and singing games (to include clapping, tapping and nodding accompaniments);
* body percussion – clapping, slapping thighs, stamping feet, tapping heads;
* tuned percussion;
* movement (marching rhythmically, running and stopping quickly);
* making sound pictures;
* making musical instruments (learning loudly/ softly, slowly/quickly);
* using a music corner (trying instruments/ looking at pictures in books and listening to tapes.

Making musical instruments will help children to understand the principles of music and making sounds. Use materials that are familiar to the children and which they can also find to make instruments with at home. Provide a selection of instruments that can be struck, shaken, scraped, plucked or blown.

Links with physical development

Large motor skills

Creative Development is closely linked to physical development as working creatively not only develops physical skills, but physical skills are in turn needed to develop creativity. For example, dancing will foster physical co-ordination, and increased physical co-ordination will enable a child to try more dance movements such as going forwards and backwards, fast or slow.

By the age of three, children have acquired the major motor skills such as walking, running and jumping. From three to six years, children will be refining these skills and developing an increasing co-ordination, particularly small muscle co-ordination. Children will be much more aware of space and will begin to be able to co-ordinate their movements to account for it. For example, they will be able to jump in and out of a hoop laid on the ground, and will be able to direct their movements in different directions, upwards, downwards, fast and slow. They are also beginning to be able to work in groups and with partners. This is the age at which they will begin to play games and to use large game equipment, such as bats and balls, and to take part happily in ring games, dances and some simple partner work.

Children will need daily opportunities to use their large muscles by running, jumping, climbing and balancing, so that they can begin to express themselves through their movements. They will be developing confidence in their movements and this will show in their use of apparatus, in an awareness of safety factors and an understanding of the way in which they can co-operate with others through movement. As they increase in confidence so they will increasingly begin to use their bodies imaginatively, for example twisting and turning when running, or bending and stretching using the space around them.

Fine motor skills

Children will also need daily opportunities to develop small muscle skills so that they can handle tools and equipment with increasing skill, such as crayons, pencils, small brushes, scissors and woodwork tools. They will need to be able to manipulate materials such as sand, pastry and clay showing an increasing awareness of texture, and as they develop greater manual dexterity they will be able to manipulate the materials in a greater variety of ways.

Children of this age experience materials and equipment through their senses and need to have a range of opportunities to feel, listen, smell, taste and see items. As they handle materials such as water, sand and earth, they show an increasing awareness of their similarities and differences and the way in which they can be used and are developing their manipulative skills. Children show an increasing skill in matching hand and eye co-ordination, for example through cutting out, threading, hammering, painting and drawing.

All creative activities involve both reflection and action, for example the children thinking what to paint and then painting it. The active elements of these activities serve to foster physical development as well as development of creative skills.

Developing movement and drama

Daily practice of these skills is important. Provide opportunities for both large scale physical play through, for example, climbing, balancing and wheeled toys, and manipulative activities, such as sand, clay and drawing. Set aside at least one area of the room for large-scale imaginative and dramatic play, so that children can try out roles and imagine themselves in different settings. Have lots of props, such as hats and bags and dressing-up clothes. Some of the most effective items are those which are not prescriptive allowing children to develop their own ideas, such as lengths of material, old curtains and pieces of ribbon which can be worn in many ways. Provide large cardboard boxes which can become 'cars', 'houses' or 'cages'. Sometimes you will want to structure these sessions by playing alongside

the children and providing some direction for example, 'Today we're going to pretend that it's a holiday and we are going on a picnic'. Children will also need regular opportunities to express their ideas and emotions in a large group through movement with music and with miming actions.

Using imagination

Children's imagination needs to be expressed through words and actions. Allow plenty of opportunities for children to discuss their ideas and to talk about their work. Help them to find the right vocabulary, encouraging them to think about descriptive words and to explain likes and dislikes. Ask questions sensitively in a way which will help them to express some of their inner feelings, such as 'How have you made the cat in your painting look so real?' or 'What does the clay feel like?'

Give children the space to talk to peers and to themselves as they work. Ensure that you provide areas of the room or times of the day when they can be noisy and behave boisterously, as well as times when they can be quiet and reflective and careful in their movements. Try to provide opportunities each day for small world and construction play where children can manipulate objects into their own scenes and pretend that laces are snakes, bricks are sandwiches and plastic counters are money!

Free expression

In setting up play, provide a careful balance between structured activities, such as teaching how to clap a rhythm, and allowing children the chance to respond in their own way. Approach children's efforts positively, saying, 'Tell me about your picture', or, 'Why have you chosen to build with these bricks?' and 'What do you like best about this model?' Support the ways they have chosen to express their ideas, be it through painting, modelling, singing or dancing. Give them time to explore materials and techniques before offering suggestions.

Similarly, try to build on a child's achievements in painting even when you can see that the child is repeating the form or figure endlessly. Encourage development by providing a change of colours to use, different tools or size of paper. Spend time talking to the child about objects, choosing something of particular interest and encourage her/him to focus on its texture, shape and colour. In this way children will develop in skill, while at the same time retaining their own ideas and self-confidence.

chapter three

Assessment and record-keeping

All good early years practitioners make assessments every day. Many assessments are done informally on a daily basis by observing how each child is responding to creative activities. These initial observations provide a good starting point for more systematic assessment.

The importance of assessment

When planning and assessing Creative Development it will be helpful to think about art, craft, music, dance and imaginative play separately to ensure that you are building up a balanced picture of each child. Children may develop at different rates in each of these aspects.

Systematic assessment will enable you to plan activities to extend the child's experience and build on the foundations of previous learning. It will also demonstrate to parents and carers, or school, how much progress she/he has made over time. This will prove the 'value added' by your provision and help you evaluate and improve your work. It will also help you to identify children who are demonstrating particular gifts, such as well developed physical/technical abilities when dancing. If progress is limited, it will help to identify children with special educational needs at an early stage so that they can receive appropriate extra help.

Inspectors will be making judgements about the quality of your provision for under fives, using the Desirable Outcomes as a basis for their evaluations. They will look at your programme of Creative Development, and how you assess and record children's attainment and progress, and how you then use assessments to plan future suitable work.

National Baseline Assessment

From September 1998, all schools in England and Wales will be required to undertake formalised 'Baseline Assessment' shortly after a child commences statutory age schooling. Schools will have to use a Baseline Assessment system which has been officially accredited by the DfEE, assessing against criteria of the Desirable Outcomes for Children's Learning.

Information from previous early years provision can be considered and parents should be involved in discussions with the school. It makes sense for your assessment procedures to match these arrangements, as it would be helpful for parents, carers and receiving schools, and would also help you develop your own good quality assessment programme.

Linking planning and assessment

It is vital that you know clearly what it is you are going to assess and when you will make the assessment. You will need to break down your plans into subsections which cover art, craft, music, dance and imaginative play to ensure balance. This will enable you to provide regular, planned coverage across the range of physical, emotional, imaginative, technical and social skills which will ensure good overall Creative Development.

Once an appropriate range and balance of activities have been built into your planning, you can decide when and how you will carry out your assessments. Identify which activities can be used for small group assessments and which for individuals. For example, a printing activity (such as 'Simple printing blocks' in Chapter 5, on page 34) will give you the chance to note individual progress. A junk modelling activity (such as 'Fun with junk', in Chapter 6, on page 46) will give you the opportunity to look at a small group of children and observe how they use materials.

The planning cycle

Long-term plans can show which activities are to be assessed. You should spread these evenly across the five subsections of Creative Development to achieve a balance. You should also choose activities and times which will enable you to record progress systematically, for example, painting should be observed for every child during each term, so that you can record what the child is painting and how they use space and colour. (See the example on page 10.)

Medium-term plans should indicate how many assessed activities are to be followed each week. One or two creative activities should be used every week for assessment purposes. If you are observing children during dance/movement one week, try to look at music the next, art the next and so on. This should give a good balance over each half-term. (See the example on page 11.)

Short-term plans should indicate when the activities are going to be observed, which children are to be included, who will be assessing them, how long the assessment will take and what form of assessment is to be used. (See the example on page 11.)

The assessment process

When to assess?

You will want to make an early assessment of each new child, after an appropriate settling in period. Some things may be noticeable right away, such as the child's interest in playing in the home corner, or a child enjoying Plasticine play. Record these initial observations as simple, informal notes for later reference. When the child has got used to the setting and daily routines, make more formal observations.

Decide on the most appropriate time to share this first assessment with parents and carers. Use this meeting as an opportunity to continue any initial discussions of what the child does at home, and to talk about their particular interests and activities which could be followed at home or at the group to promote development. For example, if a child seems worried about using scissors, a joint decision may be reached to do some cutting out activities at home.

Who assesses?

Every adult who has dealings with the children in the setting has useful contributions to make. They will need to be very clear about what is to be assessed. Provide them with written copies of the assessment sheets for each area of Creative Development, together with suggestions for ways to observe and record. These should also be discussed, particularly if people are working in the setting on a fairly infrequent basis. Contributions from parents and from outside agencies where appropriate should also be included.

How can we assess?

This can be done in several ways. Firstly, when particular children are to be assessed during an activity, the group leader will need to know exactly what and who is to be assessed, what the child must do to meet agreed targets (for example, showing an awareness of colour through using and naming blue and collecting other items which are blue); how this is to be recorded (completing a dated tick list, making notes for later recording and so on), and whether any examples of art work for example, should be kept for children's files.

Named children can be targeted on a rolling programme in order to discover how they are developing creatively. For example, two children can be selected per session and all the team asked to make notes on what creative activities the children choose, how they respond and what they achieve. At the end of the session notes can be compared and significant points can then be entered by one person onto the child's record sheets for Creative Development. Such observations can also highlight areas where skills are not being developed. For example, a child may be avoiding music related activities. When planning the next week's activities you can then ensure that some music activities are followed and assessed.

How can we record?

Have a file for each child with a sheet on all the areas of Creative Development (see the examples of assessment sheets on pages 73–76). Each of these sheets should indicate the appropriate Desirable Outcome targets to be achieved, and should be filled in regularly and updated each half-term.

Collect and date examples of art work each half-term. Choose some examples over the year that indicate a range of techniques and materials which have been used. Also collect one or two each term which show stages of drawing/writing/ painting development. Photocopies or photographs can sometimes be used if the originals cannot be kept.

Many stages of Creative Development can best be recorded through photographs with captions, in particular the children's response to movement, children engaged in imaginative play and the children's models. It is also appropriate at times to use audio tapes, for example, to record children singing, making sounds and expressing their ideas through drama.

Involving parents and carers

Parents are their child's first educators and they, and other carers, see their child in many different contexts beyond school and playgroup. Encourage parents and children to contribute some photographs or examples from home such as of a child attending an out of school dance class or a picture they have made at home.

Parents and carers should ideally be partners in their child's learning and be fully informed of the work that their child will undertake, being involved in regular discussions on the progress they make. You will need to gather important preliminary information about the child. This could be done by going on a home visit or during a child's initial visit. It is better done in a warm informal way alongside a parent, rather than by merely presenting the parent with a form to fill in. Try to personalise the form or make it part of an induction booklet that parent and child can complete together, leaving space for the child to draw a self-portrait.

During your initial meeting with the child and his/her parents/carers you could provide materials such as paper, scissors and magazine pictures, so that the child can make a picture and a small collection of interesting objects which you can talk about. These will give you an idea of the child's stage of Creative Development.

Arrange to discuss a child's progress with parents as soon after your first assessment as possible. This can be done on a rolling programme, inviting parents to stay behind for a few minutes after a session, where the child can also be involved, or at a more formalised 'open evening'. Highlight what a child can do, what they are progressing in, and select one or two targets that you and home can work on together, and explain how these are best tackled. For instance, if a child needs to develop more experience of making things you can suggest ways of making simple models from old cereal packets and boxes at home. At subsequent meetings remember to report on progress, and set new agreed targets.

It is also useful to send newsletters home which give an outline of the work the children will be covering in the next few weeks. You will then be able to report back to parents on how well their children understood and perhaps have photos, work or drawings in the child's record books or files to show them.

Keep parents informed about how they will hear of their children's progress, publish your parents' meeting schedule and explain that regular assessment is part of your everyday work. Outline the annual cycle with dates, and also explain your plans for more informal discussions – such as before and after sessions.

chapter four

Music

Young children have a natural enthusiasm for making music and singing and it is an important part of the development of their creative skills. The activities in this chapter will help children to learn about rhyme, rhythm, body percussion and how to use percussion instruments.

A rainy day

Learning outcome

To develop awareness of soft, loud and graduated sounds, stopping and starting.

Group size
Whole group.

What you need
Musical instruments, such as a drum, chime bar, shakers, bells, triangles, rhythm sticks.

Preparation
Make sure you have enough instruments for about six children to use at a time. Put the instruments in a box by your side. Sit with the children in a circle.

What to do
Begin by establishing signals for stop and start. If using hand gestures make these clear and bold, such as pointing and directing the right index finger like a baton to start and raising the right hand, palm forwards for stop. Once the children are sure of these signals practise them together by stopping and starting them as they sing or clap.

Tell the children a simple story about a rainy day, with the rain beginning slowly then building up; thunder crashing; children hurrying indoors and then rain slowly stopping.

Now take the instruments out of the box one by one and play them. Ask the children to listen closely to the sounds each one makes. Decide together which sort of rain or sound each instrument should represent. For example the rhythm sticks could be footsteps.

Choose a group of six children to have different instruments. Repeat the story, this time giving the children the chance to play the instruments in turn.

Questions to ask
What sound does the rain make? Can you think of any words to describe rain? (Note these down for future reference.) Does pouring rain sound the same as drizzle? What sort of sound does thunder make? How do you feel when it thunders? Listen while I tap the rhythm sticks, do you think that sounds like someone walking? Can you hear them walking faster/slower?

For younger children
Do the activity without the instruments, just using body percussion to create different sounds.

For older children
Give instruments to a larger group of children, so that there are two or three using each instrument. This will emphasise the sounds.

Follow-up activities
∗ Sing the song 'I hear thunder'.
∗ Make a collection of rain words and write them up on a chart.
∗ Record the sound of rain and play it for the children. When it is raining encourage the children to listen to the different rain sounds.
∗ Paint pictures of rainy days – ask the children which colours they think are 'rainy'.

Links with home

Ask parents to read stories about rainy days to their child.

Sing a song of sixpence

To develop voice control and awareness of rhyme and musical patterns

Group size
Whole group.

What you need
Old nursery rhyme books, card, scissors, glue, clear adhesive film, flip chart and large felt-tipped pen.

Preparation
Make nursery rhyme cards by cutting out the pages from old rhyme books (obtained from jumble sales, or ones that are no longer good enough for everyday use), sticking them to sheets of card and covering them with clear adhesive film. Sit near the flip chart and seat the children on the floor around you

What to do
Choose one of the cards and hold it up. See if anyone can tell you which rhyme it is. Once identified, sing the rhyme through together a couple of times. Repeat the process with some of the other cards.

Now choose a rhyme that the children are not familiar with and teach it to them. Write the first verse out on the flip chart and point to the words as you are singing it. Encourage the children to sing together and to maintain a regular rhythm, not going too fast or too slow. Look at the nursery rhyme on the chart together and say the rhyme slowly, emphasising the words that rhyme. Can they hear the rhyming words? Underline them on the flip chart. Sing the rhyme through together one last time.

Questions to ask
Which nursery rhyme do you think this is? How do you know? Can you tell me how it goes? Can you hear any words that rhyme/sound the same? Do the rhymes make a pattern?

For younger children
Write out the words to a familiar rhyme such as 'Humpty Dumpty' and underline the rhyming words. Ask the children to sing the rhyme slowly and help them to clap as they say the rhyming words – wall, fall; men, again.

For older children
Listen to some nursery rhymes on a cassette. Ask them to listen out for the rhyming words. Can they tell you what they were?

Follow-up activities
* Make a display of nursery rhyme books, pictures and cards for the children to look at. Encourage them to sing their favourite tunes.
* Set up the tape recorder and ask pairs of children to record nursery rhymes; each one singing to the other.
* Act out some of the rhymes (see 'Let's act it out', page 53).
* Make simple props for the children, such as hats, shepherd's crook, hobby horse, blackbirds pie and a tray of jam tarts, so that they can role-play nursery rhyme characters during imaginative play.

Links with home
Ask parents to tell you about the rhymes and songs that their child enjoys at home. Invite parents to come in and share them with the group.

All clap hands

Learning outcome

To develop rhythm and co-ordination skills.

Group size

Ten to twelve children.

What you need

A list of songs which can be used for clapping games, such as 'I hear thunder' and 'Hot cross buns'.

Preparation

Select sections from the songs you have chosen which are distinctive and can be clapped.

What to do

Start by clapping the children's names. Clap and say a child's name and let the children repeat it. Do this with names that have one beat first, then try names with two beats. Draw the children's attention to the number of beats. Can they hear the difference? Clap two beats and ask them to put up their hands if they think that sounds like their name. Do the same with one beat. When the children have mastered this try clapping names with more than two beats, such as Al-i-son.

Now sing and clap your chosen song with the children. Help them to listen to the rhythm and to keep up with you. Try clapping a phrase from the song which has a marked rhythm pattern such as 'hark don't you' in 'I hear thunder' and ask the children if they can guess which bit you clapped.

Questions to ask

How many beats can you hear when I clap? Can you copy my clapping pattern? How many beats has your name got? Can you clap your name to me?

For younger children

Sing and clap well-known songs and rhymes regularly encouraging the children to keep in rhythm.

For older children

Help older children to make up a clapping pattern, such as one beat, two beats, one beat, two beats and so on.

Follow-up activities

* Sing lots of action songs which involve clapping, such as 'If you're happy and you know it' and 'We all clap hands together'.
* Make some sand blocks (see 'Bells and jingles' on page 28) and let the children clap these together.
* Make cards with one dot for one beat, two dots for two beats and invite children to clap as you hold them up.
* Practise clapping quickly and slowly.

Links with home

Suggest parents play 'Pat-a-cake' with their child to develop co-ordination skills.

Tap that rhythm

Learning outcome

To develop an awareness of different sounds.

Group size
Whole group.

What you need
A few familiar songs or rhymes. One or two adult helpers to join in.

Preparation
Decide which songs you are going to use and which parts of the body you want to focus on. Consider if there are any children who will require extra help.

What to do
Sit in a circle on the carpet with the children. Make sure that the children have room to tap their feet. Begin by asking the children to clap their hands as they sing a familiar song or rhyme. Then just clap hands, varying the speed and volume.

Show the children how to make other sounds with their hands: tapping two fingers on palms; drumming the fingers of one hand on the palm of the other; clicking fingers and hitting the tips of fingers together. Demonstrate some other sounds that can be made – slapping thighs, tapping heads and tapping and stamping feet. Invite the children to have a go but remind them to be gentle!

When you have explored a few ideas work out a simple body percussion tune, such as a clap, a tap with the foot and a slap on the thigh. If children manage this well try repeating the actions twice. Sing another song, tapping the feet or clapping the knees.

Questions to ask
What sounds can we make with our hands? Can you think of any others? What sort of sound does it make if you tap your head? Make a fist and punch the other hand – tell me what it sounds like. Try to make a tune by clapping and tapping. Can you describe your tune to me?

For younger children
Ask children to use their hands to accompany familiar rhymes and songs. They could try clicking, tapping or clapping.

For older children
Make up more complex rhythms such as two taps, four claps, two clicks, two claps for the children to copy.

Follow-up activities
* Many sounds can be made by the mouth – blowing, sucking, clicking, gurgling and so on. In a small group, make the sounds and list all the different noises that can be made.
* Make a sound board by fixing different textured material such as sandpaper, sponge, rubber and velvet to a piece of strong board. Let the children tap their fingers over each material and note the differences in sound.
* Ask a tap dancer in to demonstrate how tunes can be tapped out by the feet. Ask the dancer to show the children their special shoes.
* Watch a video of Irish dancing and listen to the rhythms of the feet.

Links with home

Write out a simple body percussion sequence and ask parents to practise it at home with their child.

Musical moments

Learning outcome

To learn to appreciate a variety of styles of music and the work of well-known composers.

Group size

Six to ten children.

What you need

A cassette recorder and a selection of cassettes that reflect a variety of styles. Suggestions include: compilation tapes of particular moods like 'Tranquility'; classical extracts such as from, Debussy's *Clair de Lune*, Grieg's *Peer Gynt*, Holst's *The Planets*, or Tchaikovsky's *Nutcracker Suite*; and examples of particular instruments – piano, harp, violin, guitar, pan pipes and African drums. A quiet area of the room or separate quiet space, comfortable seating, such as a carpet area or floor cushions.

Preparation

Set up the listening space so that each child will be comfortable. Check that the cassette recorder is working and that the cassettes are ready to play.

What to do

Settle the children down and encourage them to sit quietly. Tell them that you are going to play some music for them to listen to. Tell them what sort of music it is, for example a march that is lively and exciting or a peaceful piece of ballet music.

Show the children how to listen quietly by closing your eyes and being very still. Ask the children to copy you and listen carefully to the music you are going to play. Explain that you want them to see what pictures it makes in their head. Put on the tape and play your chosen piece of music for about two to three minutes.

When the music has finished encourage the children to move vigorously for a few moments to break the tension of concentration. Then ask them to think about the pictures that they saw in their heads when they listened to the music. After a moment or two ask the children in turn to tell the group about their pictures.

Repeat the activity at another session, this time with a contrasting piece of music.

Questions to ask

How does this music make you feel? Is it peaceful/lively music? Did it make you want to dance/sing? Did you like the music? What did you like best about it? What sort of picture did the music make in your head?

For younger children

Play the music during a quiet period of the day. Encourage them to listen to the music and enjoy it with them.

For older children

Play the extracts for a little longer if they are listening attentively.

Follow-up activities

∗ Play some contrasting pieces of music – some that use different instruments and some that originate from different cultures such as piano, violin, reggae and waltzes.
∗ Take one style or one composer and play the children a selection of pieces.
∗ Tell a simple version of 'Peter and the Wolf' or 'Sleeping Beauty' and listen to small extracts of music from each.
∗ Use some music as the basis of movement sessions, encouraging the children to think carefully about how the music makes them feel.

Links with home

Let parents borrow some of the tapes to listen to with their child at home.

Bells and jingles

Learning outcome

To develop awareness of the way sounds are made.

Group size

Four children.

What you need

Eight paper plates, 24 metal curtain rings (the type that can be opened), 48 metal bottle tops (obtainable from large stores selling wine-making equipment), hole punch, paint, varnish.

Preparation

Glue two plates together for each child and ask the children to paint and varnish them on both sides in advance. Make holes in the centre of each bottle top by hammering a nail through onto a piece of wood. Put each child's plate in their space, together with 6 rings and 12 bottle tops. CARE! The children will need to be carefully supervised throughout this activity. Ensure that the bottle tops are not too sharp and make sure that the children handle them carefully.

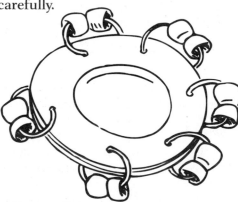

What to do

Each plate will need six holes. Using a hole punch make six evenly-spaced holes on each of the children's plates. Encourage them to count the holes with you. Each hole should be about 15mm from the edge of the plate. Make sure you are on hand to give the children assistance throughout the activity.

Show the children how to thread two bottle tops back-to-back on an open curtain ring and then clip that through one of the holes on the plate. Continue until all six holes are threaded with the curtain rings and bottle tops. S h a k e the tambourines and tell the children to listen to the jingles!

Questions to ask

How do the bottle tops make a sound? What do they sound like? Do the bottle tops make a sound when they are still? What do you need to do to play your tambourine?

For younger children

Make sand blocks by gluing pieces of sandpaper to wood offcuts. Sand down any rough edges on the wood then trim the sandpaper to fit the blocks. Fold the paper round the block lengthways and glue to three sides. Leave the top free for easy handling. Play the blocks by rubbing them together.

For older children

Make more holes in the tambourines and decorate them by threading ribbons.

Follow-up activities

* Make rhythm sticks from 15cm lengths of doweling (1.5cm thick). Cut two the same. Let the children sandpaper the ends and paint them. Play them by tapping together.
* Make clappers by gluing cotton reel handles onto the base and lid of a wooden date box. Check that there are no rough edges and sandpaper if needed.
* Dry squeezed orange and lemon halves gently in the oven. When completely dry children can bang the halves together to make a clapping sound.
* Use the instruments to accompany songs or make sound effects for stories.

Links with home

Share your ideas with parents and suggest that they make some simple instruments at home. Ask parents if they have any other ideas for making musical instruments which you could use.

Shaker fun

Learning outcome

To learn to discriminate between sounds.

Group size

Six children.

What you need

Four identical yoghurt pots, two washing-up liquid bottles, small pieces of dowelling for each bottle, two small-/medium-sized cereal boxes, glue and spreaders, masking tape. A selection of pasta, lentils, small stones, rice and paper clips. A camera and film.

Preparation

Put the pasta, lentils and so on into plastic trays and set them out in the middle of the table. Put the yoghurt pots, glue and spreaders ready on the table. Have the masking tape near you. Set up the camera so that you are ready to take photographs of the activity as you go along.

What to do

Give two of the children two yoghurt pots each. Explain that you want the containers to look the same but to sound different. Show them the different fillings to choose from and ask them to select one to put into the bottom of one of their yoghurt pots. Help the children to join their two pots together by using masking tape. Make sure that this is fastened securely.

Next give two of the other children a washing-up liquid bottle each and ask them to half-fill it with one of the fillings. Make sure that each of the pair chooses a different filling.

Give the remaining two children a cereal box each and show them how to half-fill it with a different filling. Help them to seal the ends with the masking tape. When finished, each pair of children should paint their shakers the same colour, so that they look the same, but sound different.

Invite the children to demonstrate their shakers in turn. Talk about the different sounds that they make.

Questions to ask

What sort of sound do you think the rice will make? Put a few paper-clips in the yoghurt pot and carefully shake – what sound does it make? Why do you think it sounds different in the washing-up liquid bottle? Shake this bottle. What do you think is inside it? Why do you think that?

For younger children

Concentrate on one sort of shaker using just two different fillings. Help them to hear the difference.

For older children

Make four containers of the same type, painted to look identical. Ask the children to half-fill two with rice and two with pasta. The children have to shake them and guess the pairs.

Follow-up activities

* Make shakers out of cocoa tins, fixing the lids in place.
* Mount the photos of the shaker making activity in numbered sequence so the children can look at the process.
* Make a book with children's pictures showing how you made the shakers.

Links with home

Invite parents to come in and look at the photos of the activity so that they can talk to their child about the process involved and make the shakers at home if they wish.

Fun with sounds

To develop auditory discrimination.

Group size
Four to six children.

What you need
A cardboard box containing everyday familiar objects, such as a clock, some pieces of LEGO, knife and fork, cup and saucer, scissors and paper, a rattle, a screen.

Preparation
Set up an area so that the children can be seated in front of you. Set up a chair for yourself in front and put the box of objects next to it. Put a screen behind your chair, so you can stand behind it and still face the children.

What to do
Once the children are settled explain that you are going to show them a selection of objects and make a sound with each of them.

Take out one of the objects from the box and make a sound with it. Show the children how to make the sound and let one or two of them have a turn. Repeat the process with each object, leaving one object as a surprise for later.

When the children have heard all the sounds and they have all had a turn to make one of them, put all the objects back in the box and place them behind the screen. Make sure that no one can see behind the screen and then take an object out and make the sound. Invite the children to guess what is making the sound. Repeat the process with all the objects. When they have guessed these, make the sound of the object they haven't seen and challenge them to guess what it is.

Questions to ask
What is this? What sort of sound do you think it makes? Try and make the same sound. How did you make the sound? Can you guess what is making this sound? What sort of sound is this? How do you think it is made?

For younger children
Take three instruments, such as a small bell, shaker and chime bar and hide them from view. Play each one in turn and ask them to guess which one you are playing.

For older children
Add some extra 'mystery' items to the box. Ask them to try and guess what they are.

Follow-up activities
* Make a cassette of familiar sounds such as a tap running, pouring tea, knocking at the door, letter box, radio and so on. Can the children identify the sounds?
* Play a tape of animal sounds for the children to identify. Make a set of picture cards and a board for children to match with the sounds.
* Ask the whole group to listen for a minute. At the end of the minute encourage them to tell you what they heard.
* Talk to the children about the sounds made by the things on the photocopiable activity sheet, 'Listen carefully' on page 88.

Links with home
Ask parents to make a tape of some of the everyday sounds that their child is familiar with at home.

The music shop

Learning outcome

To explore a range of instruments and to practise musical skills.

Group size

Six children.

What you need

Posters of musicians and instruments – include a range of images from different cultures. A selection of books, photographs and postcards showing instruments, musicians, dancers and singers. Musical instruments from different cultures (bought/home-made). A cassette recorder, cassettes and headphones, screens, tables, cushions, a till, telephone, play computer and screen, writing materials. Fabric lengths for display, a curtain, curtain pole, two pole fixing rings and curtain hoops. Piece of carpet, masking tape, staple gun, Blu-Tack, pins. A flip chart and thick felt-tipped pen.

Preparation

Create a clear space for the shop to be set up, away from quiet activity areas if possible. Set up some screens in position. Make up the curtain ready to slide over the pole. Have all the items to hand ready to set up the shop quickly.

What to do

Tell the children that you would like to set up a music shop in the room. Ask them to think about what it might look like and the sorts of things that might be inside it.

On the flip chart draw a simple plan of the shop, using the children's ideas. Once you have all decided on what needs to be done, allocate different jobs to pairs of children. For example, two children could set up the buying table with the till and phone and so on.

Show the children how to put up the posters and arrange the cards. Help them to put down the carpet and set up the cushions. Screw the pole hooks into each screen and arrange the curtain pole between the two screens to make an 'entrance'. The shop is now ready for customers!

Questions to ask

Have you ever been in a music shop? What do you think might be in the shop? What would you like to buy there? How does this instrument feel? What do you think it is made of? Look at the woman in the picture – what sort of instrument is she playing? Do you think she looks happy? Are those children in the picture happy singing?

For younger children

Encourage them to use the shop for imaginative play and to explore the instruments once it has been set up.

For older children

Encourage older children to use reference books to identify some of the bought instruments you have displayed. Spend plenty of time discussing the posters with them.

Follow-up activities

* Talk about different families of instruments; blown (clarinets and flutes); plucked (violin, sitar) banged (gongs, drums). Sort the instruments into sets.
* Set up role-play in the shop, so that customers come in, look at the instruments, try them out and buy them. Only play them in the shop, and limit the number of customers at any one time.
* Set up a cassette recorder in the shop so that children can record what their instruments sound like when played.
* Use photocopiable activity sheet, 'Bang the drums' on page 89.

Links with home

Lend parents some music tapes featuring different instruments to play at home and talk about the sounds.

Doh, ray, me...

Learning outcome

To develop awareness of the sounds made by different notes.

Group size

Four to six children.

What you need

Chime bars in C, D, E, F, G, A, B, C and beaters.

Preparation

Get out the E and G chime bars and leave the others to one side.

What to do

Start by clapping the children's names, one at a time. Invite the children to clap back immediately. Then sing the names, for example Anna and Alison and ask the children to sing back. Show the children how to use the chime bars to 'play' their names Anna (G,E), Alison (G,G,E). Encourage them to use two beaters and use both their hands alternately.

Help the children to take turns to play their names on the two chime bars. While the others are waiting for their turn suggest that they practise by tapping imaginary chime bars – this will help their co-ordination.

Once all the children have had a go, challenge them to try each other's names or other words of their choice. If you feel they are ready, introduce another one or two chime bars for them to experiment with.

Questions to ask

How many claps are there in your name? What other words would you like to try? Which name do you think we are playing? Can you play any tunes?

For younger children

Leave the chime bars (E and G) in the music corner and let them just try out the notes.

For older children

Make cards with the names of the notes on for the children to use. Write out a simple tune such as 'Three Blind Mice'. The first two lines are E, D, C and the third and fourth are G, F, F, E. Let the childen try to copy the notes to play the tune.

Follow-up activities

∗ Use the chime bars yourself to accompany one or two rhymes in singing sessions.
∗ Photocopy some examples of written music from song sheets and display them. Explain that when people write music they use special symbols.
∗ Encourage the children to 'write' music by putting some music paper in the drawing area with some examples of music/song sheets.
∗ Sing 'doh, ray, me' to the children, and talk about the way the notes go up the scale. Draw the notes going up the stairs and point to them as you sing.

Links with home

Ask parents to talk to their children about any instruments they see when watching television. How many times do they hear music on television in a week?

chapter five

Art

The activities in this chapter concentrate on the area of art and children will develop an awareness of shape, colour, pattern and texture. They will explore printing techniques and learn to appreciate the different styles of famous artists.

Black and white

Learning outcome

To develop an awareness of shape and pattern.

Group size
Six children.

What you need
Selection of photographs, cartoons and styles of print from different newspapers (ensure that the content is suitable for young children). Choose pieces which have a mix of upper and lower case letters, some headlines and titles and some small print. Glue and scissors for each child. Pieces of A4 sugar paper in black and white.

Preparation
Tear up the sheets into easily manageable pieces. Put out pots of glue and scissors for each child. Have the paper ready.

What to do
Give each child a selection of pieces of paper and ask them to cut out letters and photographs that they like to make a collage picture. Encourage the children to look at the styles of print, recognise letters and to notice the contrast between the black and white colours. Look at the children's choice of cut-out pieces and help them to identify any shapes or patterns that they can see in their pieces.

When they have cut out a number of pieces, help the children to think about how they want to arrange them, allowing them to stick letters randomly, upside-down or sideways if they wish. Once they are happy with their arrangement they can glue their collage to the paper.

Questions to ask
What shapes and patterns have you made? Which colours can you see? How do people in photographs look when they are only in black and white? Ask whether their collage shows up best on a white or black background.

For younger children
Let the children tear up the pieces of paper rather than using scissors. Concentrate more on the design of the collage than the letter recognition aspect of the activity.

For older children
Ask the children to cut out as many letters as they can. See if they can arrange these letters into a pattern. Emphasise the different print styles and the contrast between black on white and white on black.

Follow-up activities
∗ Make a book with some examples of the different newspaper titles and typefaces used.
∗ Make a 'black and white' table with a collection of things in those colours.

Links with home
Ask children to bring in examples of black and white print and items from home for the black and white table.

Simple printing blocks

To develop an awareness of pattern making and design.

Group size
Six children.

What you need
Thin polystyrene tiles (about 30cm square), thick pencils with points that are not too sharp, trays of pre-mixed paint or printing ink, rollers and sheets of paper, aprons.

Preparation
Cut up the tiles into shapes for the children to use – 10cm squares will be easiest, but other shapes are effective. If you are using paint, mix up three small trays of paint (use baking trays if you do not have professional trays) with different colours. The paint should be fairly thick, so that it doesn't drip, and can easily be rolled. Put these in the centre of the table for children to share. Printing inks can simply be squeezed into the trays and put out in the same way. Cover a table and place a pencil, roller and piece of tile ready for each child. Put the paper ready on a table near by. Allocate somewhere to put the finished prints to dry. Ask the children to each put on an apron.

What to do
Give each child their tile and ask them to draw a pattern or picture on the tile. Ask them not to press too deeply so as not to go through the tile. This then forms their printing block.
Show each child how to roll their roller in one of the paint trays, taking care not to get too much paint on it. Ask them to roll the roller over the design on the printing block, turn over the block and then print it onto the paper. This can be done several times without needing to add fresh paint. Encourage the children to start at one corner of the paper and print their block several times to form a pattern.

Questions to ask
What do you think will happen when you start to draw on the tile? Do you think all the lines will come out? Why? How can you make your pattern more than once? Is each pattern the same? Why is that? Tell me what happens to the colour. Why does that happen? What happens if you put too much paint on the roller? Describe the pattern you have made.

For younger children
Encourage the children to draw pictures on their tiles and print them without having to make repeating patterns. Let them enjoy the experience of making prints from their own designs.

For older children
Suggest that the children design an abstract pattern or stylised form, such as a leaf or flower shape. Draw these on square tiles so that they can tessellate. Print rows of the design using different colours, such as a row of red then a row of green.

Follow-up activities
∗ Make a book of the children's designs and patterns.
∗ Mount some of the pictures and patterns in paper 'frames' so that they look like works of art.
∗ Let children make two or three blocks and print them in random patterns.
∗ Use block prints to make cards.
∗ Try drawing on the tiles with other implements, such as LEGO bricks or clay tools and experimenting with the effect.

Links with home

Ask parents to look around their homes with their child and talk about some of the patterns they see, such as curtains, carpet patterns or bathroom tiles.

Oranges and lemons

Learning outcome

To develop an awareness of the way repeat patterns are made.

Group size

Four to six children.

What you need

Four paint trays, paint in citrus colours (ready-mixed paint is about the right thickness). Oranges and lemons cut in half. Paper for printing on, aprons, newspaper.

Preparation

Cover the table with newspaper. Pour some of the paint into paint trays. Set out the table with the paint trays in the centre and an orange and lemon half for each child. Ask each child to put on an apron and put a sheet of paper in front of each child.

What to do

Show the children how to hold the fruit half carefully and dip it into the paint tray. Explain that they do not need too much paint on the fruit. Surplus paint can be removed by wiping the fruit against the edge of the paint tray.

Show them how to print with the fruit half and ask them to do repeat prints with one fruit and one colour to begin with. Then allow the children to use an extra colour to create a new repeating pattern.

When the children are confident with making a simple pattern, allow them to use more colours and both fruits. Encourage them to experiment with some patterns of their own.

Questions to ask

Tell me how your pattern goes. What comes next? How many colours did you use? Tell me what the pattern of the orange looks like. Which colour do you like best? Have you got a favourite pattern? Can you tell me why?

For younger children

Limit the printing to using just one or two colours. Allow them time to experiment with making marks on the paper and don't insist on pattern making. Let them print first using apples which are firmer to hold.

For older children

Use the oranges and lemons to design repeat patterns for wallpaper or wrapping paper. If you have access to fabric paints then these designs can be printed on fabric such as cotton or linen.

Follow-up activities

* Use some of the patterns as wallpaper for the home corner or to decorate a doll's house.
* Print with other fruits and vegetables. See which ones print most clearly and discuss why.
* Let the children make sequence patterns as borders around your wall displays.
* Make cards with sequence patterns on for children to copy. These can vary in level of difficulty.

Links with home

Invite parents in to see the children's printing work. Suggest that they try printing at home with pieces of potato, cut into shapes.

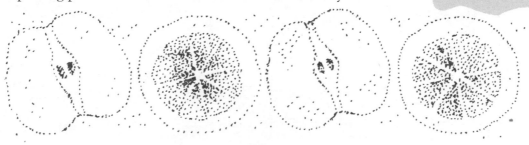

Exploring seeds

Learning outcome

To explore the textures and colours of a variety of seeds and pulses.

Group size

Four to six children.

What you need

Pieces of A4 dark-coloured sugar paper, small pots of white glue (one between two children) and a spreader per child, newspaper, paper towels. Small trays each containing a different type of seed or pulse. Use several types of lentil and split peas, sesame seeds, melon seeds, sycamore seeds, acorns, conkers and so on.

Preparation

Cover a large table with newspaper and set up the trays and pots. Make sure that children have easy access to a place to wash and dry their hands. Have paper towels to hand.

It is very important to ensure that none of the seeds are poisonous, for example, do not use red kidney beans. Also be sure to supervise the activity closely. Stress that the children should not try and eat the seeds or put them in their nose or ears.

What to do

Allow the children plenty of time to look at the seeds and to feel them and discuss them, exploring the textures and colours. Ask them to choose a selection of seeds to make up a pattern or picture.

Help them to spread their glue thinly onto their piece of paper and press the seeds carefully into position.

Questions to ask

How does that seed feel? What sort of shape is it? Try to extend the children's vocabulary by using words such as, hard, soft, spiky, rough, sharp, smooth and slippery. Encourage the children to describe the seeds in their own way, expressing their ideas, such as 'this feels like velvet'. When they have finished their pictures ask them to talk about their picture to the others.

For younger children

Give younger children smaller pieces of paper so that they can achieve results more quickly.

For older children

Draw a picture, such as a flower or plant, photocopy it and invite the children to complete the picture by sticking on some seeds.

Follow-up activities

∗ Encourage the children to group the seeds into sets and stick them onto sheets with labels.
∗ Make cards for special occasions using the seeds to make patterns.
∗ Collect seeds in the Autumn and set up a display table.
∗ Plant some seeds and watch them grow.

Links with home

Ask parents to talk to their child about seeds they use for cooking, or in gardening.

Colourful crayons

Learning outcome

To encourage the imaginative use of colour and design.

Group size

Four children.

What you need

A variety of crayons in different sizes, colours and thicknesses. Paper in different sizes and colours. Small items, such as coins or leaves which can be used for rubbings.

Preparation

Put a selection of crayons into small pots; one pot for each child. Put the items for rubbing in a box in the centre of the table with the pile of paper.

What to do

Talk with the children about the different colours of crayons and paper. Let them choose which colours they would like to try. Encourage them to talk about the effects of colours on different-coloured backgrounds.

Show the children the items you have selected for making rubbings. Show them how to make a rubbing, explaining that they must choose an item and place it carefully under the paper. Ask the children to hold it carefully in place and rub the crayon across the top, using the side rather than the tip of the crayon.

Questions to ask

Which crayons are easiest to use? How can you make your colours look soft? How can you make the colours hard? What happens when you rub over the piece of paper with a coin underneath? Can you scratch the crayon off with your finger? What happens when you crayon one colour on top of another?

For younger children

Younger children will enjoy drawing on very large sheets of paper which can be put on the floor, or cover a whole table with a piece of paper for crayoning on and allow a group of children to draw on it together.

For older children

Ask the children to draw a picture using thick crayons to create bold outlines. Then let them brush a thin wash of paint all over the picture. The crayons will resist the paint leaving a clear design against a painted background.

Follow-up activities

∗ Do washes over the crayon pictures with coloured inks instead of paint.
∗ Take the children outside to do some rubbings, such as brick and fence patterns.
∗ Let the children make stripy pictures by colouring in bands of colour starting with the darkest colour and gradually getting lighter.

Links with home

Ask parents to encourage their child to use crayons at home to draw a picture of something which they really like. Ask them to bring in their pictures and make a display.

Blot painting

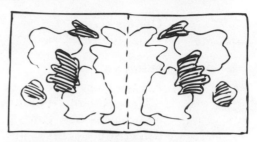

Learning outcome

To develop understanding of colour and symmetry.

Group size

Six children.

What you need

Paper, paints in about eight different colours, mixed to a fairly thick consistency, brushes, aprons.

Preparation

Ensure there is plenty of room for thechildren to spread out as they work. Mix up paints in pots with a brush in each pot. Give each child a sheet of paper and have a pile of extra paper ready. Make sure the children are wearing aprons.

What to do

Put the paint pots in the centre of the table so all the children can reach them. Show the children how to place blobs of paint down one side of the paper. Then show them how to fold the paper over, pressing down carefully over all areas of the paper. The paper should then be carefully opened up to reveal a symmetrical pattern. Discuss the way in which the pattern on each side of the paper is the same and talk about the way the colours have merged.

Questions to ask

Which colours are you going to use? What happens if this colour mixes with this one? What do you think will happen to the colours when we fold the paper? Why do we need to press down all over the paper? What has happened now? Are the two sides the same? What sort of pattern have you made?

For younger children

Encourage them to experiment with a range of colours, talking about their favourites and naming the colours as they use them. Draw attention to the way the colours change as they are mixed by the folding process.

For older children

Encourage children to create symmetrical patterns by placing the blobs of paint more deliberately in sections on one side of the paper and concentrating on the pattern making. Suggest that they experiment with placing colours at the edges and the centres and discuss how this affects their pattern.

Follow-up activities

* Look at symmetrical patterns in nature such as butterflies' and birds' wings.
* Use photocopiable page 90 to develop the children's understanding of symmetry. Ask them to complete the pictures to make them symmetrical.
* Cut out the symmetrical patterns in the paintings and mount them. Many can be mounted as butterflies suspended from the ceiling.
* Mix the paint up thicker/thinner and discuss the differences in the way the paint spreads.
* Set up a table with mirrors and items so that children can look at symmetrical images.
* Create a pattern with crayons on one half of a sheet of A4 paper and ask children to copy the pattern on the other half. Do the same using cut-out pieces of sticky paper.

Links with home

Ask parents to help their child to find examples of symmetrical patterns in their homes or gardens, such as designs on tiles or carpets.

Straw patterns

Learning outcome

To develop a creative response to random pattern making and irregular shapes.

Group size

Four children.

What you need

Drinking straws, A4 sheets of sugar paper, scissors, powder paint in four different colours, shallow containers or deep palettes, droppers to apply paint, newspaper, aprons.

Preparation

Cover the table with newspaper. Mix up the powder paint to a fairly watery consistency and pour into shallow containers or deep palettes. Arrange one dropper for each colour. Give each child a straw and ensure that they are wearing an apron.

What to do

Show children how to squeeze the dropper so that it picks up the paint; how to carefully move the dropper over the paper and then squeeze it again so that a drop or two of paint is released onto the paper. Ask the children to keep each dropper with its own colour paint. Ask the children to drop some blobs of paint onto their own piece of paper. Then show them how to blow carefully through their straws to move the paint around. Discuss the patterns and shapes that the children have made.

Supervise the activity closely at all times to ensure that the children do not suck paint up the straws and only blow.

Questions to ask

Have you ever seen or used a dropper before? Do you know how it works? Can you see the paint rising in the tube? Why do you think that is happening? What will happen when you squeeze the dropper over the paper? What is happening to the colours? Describe your picture to me.

For younger children

Use brushes instead of droppers to put blobs of paint onto the paper.

For older children

Give the children round pieces of paper on a round tin tray. Show the children how they can carefully spin their tray round with one hand so that the colours splay out as they are blown through the straw.

Follow-up activities

∗ When the pictures are dry let children draw on top of them with black crayon or a thin black felt-tipped pen.
∗ Make pictures in 'sea' colours – blue, green and turquoise and use them to make the underwater background for a sea frieze.
∗ Ask children to make a 'fire' picture using orange, red and yellow.
∗ Make a collection of words to describe the shapes and patterns that the children can see, such as, 'creepy', 'squiggly' and 'patchy'.

Links with home

Show parents how random patterns can be made using felt-tipped pens on paper towels which are very slightly damp, so they can make patterns at home.

Marbling fun

Learning outcome

To develop imagination and awareness of colour, shape and pattern.

Group size
Six children.

What you need
Aprons, marbling inks in several colours, a deep plastic tray (a new cat litter tray is ideal), droppers for each colour ink, a supply of A4 paper – printing or photocopying paper gives the best results.

Preparation
Ask the children to put aprons on. Fill the plastic tray with clean water. Set up the table with the water tray in the middle and the marbling inks and droppers nearby. Make sure that you have a clear flat surface nearby to dry off the finished prints.

What to do
Show the children how to put the dropper into the ink bottle, squeeze it and pick up the ink. Squeeze a drop or two into the tray. Repeat using two or three colours. Watch as the ink spreads out over the surface of the water.

Help the children to gently lay a piece of paper over the surface of the water for a few seconds. Make sure that all of the paper is in contact with the water. Carefully remove the paper by lifting from one of the corners and trying not to get finger marks on it. The marbling design will be clearly visible on the underside of the paper. Leave it to dry. Several prints can be taken from the same pattern before you need to add any more drops of ink, in fact often the best prints are the ones with only a light coating of colour. Always add ink sparingly, as it will congeal if there is too much.

Questions to ask
Encourage the children to think about the way that the colours change and mix. What do you think will happen when you put the ink into the water? Why has the ink spread out? Which colour spreads faster? Why hasn't that bit of ink mixed in? Children will be delighted with the patterns so encourage them to talk about their feelings and to describe what they see. What does the water look like now? Which colours do you like best?

For younger children
Demonstrate the technique to younger children letting them enjoy watching and talking about the process. Record some of the comments the children make and list the colours they can see on a flip chart.

For older children
Encourage older children to experiment using different types of paper – glossy, matt, thick, thin, light and dark and compare the results. Which paper produces the best patterns?

Follow-up activities
* Choose a selection of the marbled prints. Arrange them in a mini art gallery. Ask the children to describe the patterns and colours that they can see and to say why they like particular prints.
* Use the prints as covers for individual or group books.
* Use the marbled prints as background mounts for the children's photographs.
* Find out how many times a print can be taken from the tray (without renewing the ink) before the pattern completely disappears.

Links with home

Use the marbled prints to cover home-made boxes for the children to give to someone in their family.

Our art gallery

Group size
Whole class.

What you need

An easel, a pen and some paper, a selection of postcards and prints showing paintings from a number of artists based on a theme, such as animals, flowers or children. Choose a selection which are quite distinctly different from each other if possible. Books about some of the artists showing a further selection of pictures. Try to get at least four pictures which are A3 or larger so that children can see them clearly.

Preparation

Sit the children comfortably on a carpet if possible. Set up an easel facing the children to display the pictures on. Sit beside it and have the books and postcards to hand.

What to do

Introduce the discussion by talking briefly about the theme you are focusing on, for example, animals. Have one print ready on the easel (say of a lion), but at this stage keep it covered with a couple of sheets of paper. Ask the children what they think a lion looks like and note on the paper some of the main features that they suggest. Then uncover the print and check it against their comments.

Show the children two or three more pictures on the same theme, by different artists. Ask the children to talk about what they can see in the pictures. Encourage them to compare the different styles.

Questions to ask

Does the lion look like you expected? What can you see in the picture which is surprising? What else can you see in the picture besides the lion? How do you think he feels? Why do you think that? Do you think that the person who painted this was happy/sad? Why do you think that? Ask the children which painting they liked best. Can they tell you why?

For younger children

Have a set of postcards showing artists' paintings on a similar theme and encourage them to talk to you and to each other about the pictures, just as they might with a book.

For older children

Work in small groups, give each child a postcard and ask them to find all the colours that the artist has used. Ask an adult to write down their lists.

Follow-up activities

* Set up a themed display table with the prints, postcards and books that you are looking at. Add some artefacts, such as examples of different types of paints, a palette and brushes that might have been used.

* Focus on the work of one artist and look at a range of their work, displaying some copies of their work.

* Let children choose their favourite picture and invite them to paint their own version using the same colours.

* Choose one picture and make a list of all the things which children can see in it.

* Choose some examples of abstract paintings and ask children to find all the shapes that they can.

* Make a class book containing postcards of the children's favourite pictures. Under each picture let the children dictate a line for you to write about why they like that particular one.

Flour paste patterns

Learning outcome

To develop awareness of pattern, texture and design, and to develop manipulative skills and tactile awareness.

Group size

Four to six children.

What you need

A table with a smooth, washable surface or pieces of lino/mats to work on. Flour, water and a jug to mix them in. Powder paint and a large spoon. Kitchen paper, aprons, a nearby bowl of water and paper towels.

Preparation

Make sure the table surface is clean. If you are using place mats or lino boards to work on, put one in each child's place. Put the flour and water into the jug in roughly equal amounts and mix to a thick, smooth paste, adding more water or flour as needed to get the right consistency. Add the powder paint to colour the paste. Put a spoonful of paste in each child's place. Ask each child to put on an apron.

What to do

Share the paste mixing process with the children, so that they can look at the changes in consistency and colour. Let the children use the paste to make patterns and pictures with their fingers. They will enjoy making pictures and then wiping them out with more finger movements. If they wish to keep a particular picture, show them how they can take a print by laying a sheet of kitchen paper over the top of the paste picture and pressing down carefully. Show them how to remove the paper to reveal their monoprint.

Make sure that the children wash their hands at the end of the activity.

Questions to ask

How do you think the paste is going to feel? How does it feel? What happens to your picture as you move your fingers? What can you change your picture into?

For younger children

Let younger children enjoy the experience of moving their fingers around in the paste. Encourage them to talk about how it feels. Suggest that they make pictures with one finger or thumb at a time to develop their manipulative skills.

For older children

Suggest that they write in the paste, using as many letter shapes as they can think of.

Follow-up activities

∗ Make patterns in the paste using pieces of card cut into 'comb' shapes.
∗ Make up paste in thinner and thicker mixtures and invite the children to describe how each one feels and which they like best.
∗ Set up a 'feely' table with a collection of items for children to touch.
∗ Make a feely box – cutting a hole in the side of a cardboard box so children can put their hands inside to feel different textures. Try handfuls of hay, dried leaves, a piece of velvet or a ripe tomato!

Links with home

Ask parents to talk to their child about the different textures that they can find in the home. How many smooth things can they find?

chapter six

Craft

In the craft activities in this chapter the children will learn how to use a range of materials, tools, instruments and other resources to express ideas and communicate their feelings.

Unbreakable plates

Learning outcome

To understand how materials can be joined and hardened for extended use.

Group size
Four to six children.

What you need
Sheets of old newspaper, a large pack of wallpaper paste without fungicide, a jug of water, bowl and spoon for mixing, a brush and a plate for each child, paints, varnish, aprons.

Preparation
Mix up the paste with the water to a fairly thick consistency. Tear up the sheets of newspaper into sizes which the children can handle. Ask each child to put on an apron and give each child a brush and some newspaper. Put the bowl of paste in the centre of the table.

What to do
Show the children how to tear up the paper randomly into small pieces about the size of a credit card. When they have a pile of small pieces in front of them, give each child a plate and show them how to use the brush to paste on a piece of paper over the plate, starting at the edge and keeping to the shape of the plate. Show them how to paste on the other pieces overlapping them slightly so that the plate is covered with one layer.

Repeat the process until each child has six layers. Leave to dry. Once dry and hard the paper 'plate' can be gently removed from the original plate, painted, decorated and varnished.

Questions to ask
How many pieces do you think you will need to cover the plate? How does the newspaper feel? How does it feel when it is covered with paste? What do you think will happen when the papier mâché dries? Will we be able to get it off the plate? How long do you think it will take to dry? What do you think it will feel like then?

For younger children
Younger children will enjoy the experience of tearing up pieces of newspaper and this will help to develop their manipulative skills. They will need some help to stick the pieces of paper carefully onto the plate.

For older children
Show them how to mix up the paste and pieces of paper in a bucket to a very thick papier mâché pulp, which can then be moulded. Give each child a lump of the mixture to mould into a round, tennis ball size shape. This can later be painted, decorated and used for throwing and catching.

Follow-up activities
∗ Use papier mâché pulp to make puppet heads, pinching out the facial features and making a neck which can later be attached to a cloth puppet.
∗ Make a tea set with papier mâché cups, saucers and plates in the same patterns.
∗ Show a plate with the Willow Pattern design and read the poem on page 77.

Links with home

Ask parents to look at the designs on their crockery at home with their child.

Moulding materials

To find out about pattern and texture and how some materials can be moulded.

Group size
Four children.

What you need
Plaster of Paris, a jug of water, old spoons, several foil trays about 14cm × 8cm × 4cm or round cheese box lids (these are shallower, so use shallow objects). Newspaper, aprons, a selection of small items to make the casts from such as leaves, cones, sycamore seeds or shells with clear patterns.

Preparation
Spread the newspaper over the table. Give each child a foil tray or a box lid and ask them to put on an apron. Place the selection of items in the middle of the table for children to choose from. Put the plaster of Paris, spoons and the jug of water in a space near you ready to mix.

What to do
Ask each child to choose an item. Encourage them to look closely at it and talk about its shape, texture and any patterns or markings they can see. Explain that they are going to make a cast of the item. Mix up the plaster of Paris and the water to a thick but pourable consistency. Tell the children to put their objects into the centre of their trays and then pour over the plaster of Paris until the object is covered. Leave to set for about 30 minutes. When hard remove the foil tray or box lid to reveal the object set in the plaster. Remove the object to reveal the cast. Display the cast next to the original item and discuss the similarities and differences.

Questions to ask
What sort of patterns can you see on your object? Close your eyes and feel it. Tell me how it feels. What do you think will happen when I pour on the plaster?

For younger children
Let the children pour plaster of Paris into commercially made moulds such as plastic lolly trays. Insert lolly sticks before pouring in the plaster to make plaster lollies for imaginative play.

For older children
Make a hand print in the sand tray by pressing down firmly in wet sand. Surround the hand print with a cardboard collar, pressed into the sand around the print. Pour plaster of Paris into the 'mould'. Leave to set then remove the cast and take off the collar. The hand print will be revealed.

Follow-up activities
∗ Make ice-cubes using water poured into ice tray moulds. Freeze and then tip out. If you have an old ice-cube tray make some plaster 'ice-cubes' for imaginative play.
∗ Make jellies and blancmanges in moulds and turn out so that the mould patterns are revealed.
∗ Make small cakes in tins with patterns on the bottom. Show how the underside of each cake has the pattern on it.
∗ Make a collection of moulds – many old and unusual ones can be bought cheaply at antique fairs or car boot sales, such as, butter, cheese, chocolate and jelly moulds.
∗ Make moulds by pressing items, such as LEGO bricks into Plasticine in small trays and then fill with plaster.

Make a book

Learning outcome

To develop an awareness of fixing, joining, size and shape.

Group size

Two children.

What you need

Thick A4 or A5 card, book binding tape (for a zigzag book).

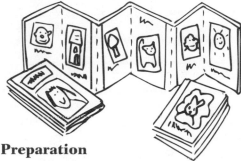

Preparation

Home-made books can be about anything you choose. They may be used for stories, to record events and experiments or may relate directly to the children's personal experiences. Decide what you wish your book to be about, then sort out how many pieces of card you will need and whether you want to use one or both sides of the card. Keep the materials by you until you are ready to start.

What to do

Give each child two pieces of card and help them to line them up next to each other leaving a gap of about a centimetre between them. Cut a length of tape approximately 6cm longer than the length of the card and help the children to join the two pieces of card together. Show them how to fold the excess tape over each end of the cards. Cut another piece of tape and help children to stick this over the overlapping tape ends to reinforce the spine. Repeat the process adding more cards to make a zigzag book.

Questions to ask

How many pages do you want in your book? Would you like pictures on both sides? How do you think we can join the card together? What materials do you think we will use? How can we make the pages bend? How can we make it stand up? Do you think it will be strong?

For younger children

Ask children to cut out pictures they have drawn or from magazines and to stick them onto both sides of strong A4 paper. Put these sheets of paper inside plastic wallets. When you have several wallets ready, help children to put on a slide-on binder to complete the book.

For older children

Make ringed books by punching holes in pieces of card and clipping them together with steel binding rings (available from stationers). Have some ready for the children to use. Sometimes it will be better for the children to mount and laminate their work first before binding the pages together.

Follow-up activities

* Make sewn books with older children. Make covers by joining two pieces of card with book binding tape (as for zigzag book). Cut four pieces of sugar paper slightly smaller than the size of the cover and fold. Open out the fold and sew through the fold, securing the pages. Glue the first and last pages to the inside of the cover.
* Make books in a range of sizes. Pocket-sized zigzag books can be made by folding paper backwards and forwards like a fan.
* Make a zigzag book with pages showing a photo of each child in the group.
* Use zigzag books to make timelines, showing photographs and pictures of the children when they were babies, toddlers and three/four years old.
* Make a table-top display showing all the books that the children have made.
* Set up a book-making area where children can make books on their own. Supply paper, card, pens, pencils, clips, staples, glue, paste, tape, a hole punch and treasury tags and let the children experiment to make their own books.

Links with home

Make a scrapbook for each child to take home and use for sticking in pictures and scraps.

Fun with junk

Learning outcome

To develop skills of fixing, joining and creative modelling.

Group size

Six to eight children.

What you need

A collection of boxes and cartons in various sizes, cylinders, small pieces of card and coloured art paper, scissors, various materials for fixing such as paste, glue, tape, paper-clips, pipe cleaners and a stapler. Yoghurt pots, paste brushes and glue spreaders.

Preparation

Use a large table. Put a carton on the floor near to the table full of the various boxes and put a small selection on the table, together with the pieces of card and the fixing materials. Put glue or paste into yoghurt cartons with brushes/spreaders.

What to do

Show the children the selection of boxes and the materials for fixing them together. Explain that they can use any of the boxes to make a model of their choice. Make some suggestions based on the theme you are working on, such as toys or transport and ask the children to come up with some ideas of their own.

Allow the children to experiment and try things out for themselves, but be on hand to help them with any difficulties they are having. Give them guidance on using the fixing materials, helping them learn how to use them correctly.

Questions to ask

Which boxes do you think you might use? What is the name of the shape? How are you going to join it? Do you want your model to bend/move? When do you think it is best to use paste? Let the children know that they can ask if they need any help.

For younger children

Give them a copy of the photocopiable sheet on page 91 and help them to cut out the pictures. Show them how to paste the shapes onto a carton or box to make windows, doors or patterns.

For older children

Limit the range of junk materials to cylinders of various sizes, for example, and challenge them to make a more specific model.

Follow-up activities

∗ Make a wall display of houses or other buildings that the children have made, creating them into a 'street'.
∗ Use some of the models such as cars, trains or houses for imaginative play.
∗ Use a number of very large boxes to make a life-size model.
∗ Experiment with different thicknesses and mixtures of paint to see which is the most effective for painting the boxes, (try mixing paint with flour, paste, washin-up liquid or PVA glue).

Links with home

Ask the children to collect old boxes and cartons from home and to bring them in each week. Ask parents to talk to their child about the shapes of the boxes, using the relevant vocabulary such as cubes, cylinders and cuboids.

Receding shapes

Learning outcome

To develop an awareness of pattern and shapes.

Group size

Six children.

What you need

A4 sheets of sugar paper, tray, glue, yoghurt pots and spreaders, pieces of card pre-cut into various sizes of rectangle (enough for ten per child).

Preparation

Put all the card rectangles into a tray in the centre of the table. Put the glue into yoghurt pots.

What to do

Give each child a sheet of sugar paper, a pot of glue and a spreader. Ask them to choose a card rectangle and stick it onto their paper. Suggest that they use the largest rectangles first. Show them how to add more rectangles, overlapping them and sticking them on top of each other, so that a pattern is built up in layers.

Questions to ask

What shapes are we using? Can you build up your shapes putting them on top of each other like bricks? Which one is the largest/smallest? Tell me what patterns you can see. How does your picture feel when you run your fingers over it?

For younger children

Give younger children smaller pieces of paper and five pre-cut pieces of card in different sizes. Help them to order the card by size and then to stick them on in order with the largest at the bottom.

For older children

Encourage older children to be more systematic with their patterns. Ask them to describe how they would like their pattern to look before they start to make it. Use the opportunity to develop comparative vocabulary, such as smaller, bigger and so on.

Follow-up activities

* Use the finished pictures to make rubbings. Cover each with a sheet of kitchen paper, hold down carefully and rub over with wax crayons.
* Make prints by using the pictures as printing blocks. Use a roller to roll paint over the surface and then take a print using kitchen paper.
* Make pictures using other shapes, such as circles, hexagons and diamonds.
* Look at examples of collage work done by different artists such as Matisse and Picasso.

Links with home

Ask parents to bring in examples of items made of paper, such as kitchen towel, tissue, writing paper. Suggest that they make a paper collage at home with their child.

Tiling patterns

Learning outcome

To develop awareness of texture, shape and size and to develop manipulative skills.

Group size
Six children.

What you need

Good quality modelling clay which can be fired, rollers, blunt knives for cutting straight lines, various implements to make the patterns, aprons, a kiln (optional), a small pot of water. Bowls of water, soap and paper towels (or a sink area if possible).

Preparation

Site the clay table away from other activities and near to a sink if possible. Use a table that can be wiped clean afterwards. Have a pot of water available to moisten the clay should it become dry during use. Ask each child to put on an apron. Divide the clay into six and give each child a piece and a roller. Put the pattern-making implements in the centre of the table.

What to do

Encourage the children to mould the clay for a while in order to get the feel of the material and to become aware of the way it can be manipulated.

Help the children to roll out the clay to a thickness of about 1cm. Then help them to cut out a tile shape using a blunt knife. Let them choose which pattern-making tools they would like to use to make their designs. Show them how to press the tools into the surface of their tile.

If possible, fire the tiles or simply allow them to harden.

Questions to ask

What happens to the clay when you squeeze it? How many lines will we need to make a square? What are you going to use to make your pattern? What design will you make?

For younger children

Just let younger children freely explore the clay, asking them questions about how the clay feels and how it responds to the way they handle it.

For older children

Let older children make several tiles. Encourage them to try and make them the same size. Suggest that they decorate them in pairs, so that they can then sequence them in a pattern such as spots, then stripes and so on.

Follow-up activities

* Make small tiles for mosaic pictures.
* Make a tile as a teapot stand.
* Make round tiles for coasters using a cutter.
* Collect examples of Islamic tile patterns.

Links with home

Encourage parents to talk to their child about tiles in their home – in the kitchen, bathroom, on the roof and so on.

Fruit feast

To develop manipulative skills and knowledge of solid shapes.

Group size
Six children.

What you need
3kg flour, salt, a jug of water, spoons, a large mixing bowl, six small pastry boards, clay tools or pencils to use when decorating. A selection of fruit such as apples, strawberries, tangerines, star fruit, mangoes and lychees. One or two books with photographs of other fruits.

Preparation
Make the dough by mixing the flour, water and salt (approximately four cups of flour to one cup of salt and one and a half cups of water).Make up the full amount and then divide the mixture into six pieces. Give each child a piece of dough and a board. Put the tools, fruit and books in the centre of the table.

What to do
Begin by passing the fruit around the children for them to look at. Encourage them to look closely at their shapes, colours and textures. Ask them to talk about what they have found out. Discuss how the fruits taste and smell. Look at some of the pictures in the books together, so that children are aware of a good variety.

Ask each child to decide on a fruit and help them to mould their dough into the relevant shape. Show them how to use the tools to make patterns on the peel or skin and at the tops and bottoms of the fruit.

Leave the dough fruits to harden for a couple of days. They can then be painted using the appropriate colours.

Questions to ask
What is the name of your piece of fruit? What shape is it? What colour is it? Describe the patterns you can see on your fruit. Can you tell me what your fruit tastes like? What is your favourite fruit?

For younger children
Choose round fruits for the children to make, as they will find round fruits easier to make and manipulate.

For older children
Ask two or three children to work together to make a bunch of grapes. Explain that they must each make a pile of grapes and then work as a team to join them together as a bunch.

Follow-up activities
* Make sets of vegetables in the same way.
* Make trays from old cereal boxes. Cut away one of the large sides, tape up the lid and fill with scrunched up tissue paper. Arrange the fruit on top.
* Have a fruit-tasting session and find out the children's favourites.
* Make a chart of the children's favourite fruits and vegetables.
* Sing songs and read poems about fruit and vegetables.

Links with home

Ask parents to make a list of all the fruit and vegetables that they usually buy each week. Encourage them to talk to their child about what they have bought, looking at all the similarities and differences between different types.

The mad hatter

Group size

Four children.

What you need

Coloured art paper, sugar paper, foil, crêpe paper, gummed paper squares, scissors, glue, pots and spreaders. A selection of collage materials to decorate the hats, such as pieces of fabric, sequins, lace, buttons and beads. Trays, stapler and tape, a selection of photographs/cards showing various hats.

Preparation

Put the collage materials into trays. Cut up some strips of crêpe paper to be used for ribbons and bows or 'tails'. Cut up some of the gummed squares and foil pieces. Cut out some basic hat shapes using the sugar paper and art paper such as headbands, crowns and cones, and some rectangular pieces with tops and brims to make a basic straw hat shape.

What to do

Show the children the hats in the pictures and talk about them – the shapes, colours and decorations. Now show the children the basic hat shapes you have prepared and ask them to choose which one they would like to make. When they have chosen their hat shape invite them to decorate it. Tell them that they can use any of the materials and help them to cut the fabric if this proves difficult.

When the children finish decorating their hats, help them to join them together using tape or stapling them to make them the right size. Hats with tops and brims are more difficult to join. Cut nicks about 2cm long,

bending the 2cm pieces down and gluing them inside the main section of the hat. Add any 'ribbons' as required.

At the end of the session invite the children to wear their hats in a hat parade.

Questions to ask

What sort of hat would you like to make? Which materials are you going to use to decorate it? Is the front of your hat going to look the same as the back? How do you think we can fix on the brims/ribbons? How can we join your hat together? When you are wearing your hat who will you pretend to be?

For younger children

Make one shape of hat only and focus the activity on decorating the hats with a variety of materials.

For older children

If children have had some experience of making hats then set up the activity without pre-cut hat shapes, so that the children can experiment with their own ideas and cut their own hat shapes out.

Follow-up activities

✳ Set up a display of hats pinning them up as a wall display. How many types you can find?
✳ Make a hat shop in the home corner for imaginative play, using some of the hats the children have made.
✳ Ask a local police or fire officer to come in and talk about the special hats that they wear.
✳ Use photocopiable page 92 as a discussion point and ask the children to match the hats to the right people.

Cards for all occasions

Group size

Six to eight children.

What you need

Pieces of card, A4 size and smaller, pencils, crayons or pens, scissors, glue, materials for collage designs such as doilies, lace, gummed paper squares, small pieces of gold and silver foil and pressed leaves.

Preparation

Fold the card over to make card shapes. Cut a few into ovals, circles and heart shapes. Set out the collage items on plastic or foil trays. Make some examples of cards using the different decorative techniques which the children could copy.

What to do

Explain to the children that there are many different ways to design a card. Tell them that you are going to show them some of the ways and then they can choose which one they would like to try. Discuss how we give cards for all sorts of different occasions and tell the children that they can choose what their card will be for. Demonstrate some of the ways to make a card, choosing one or two suggestions from the list below:

∗ draw a design with pencil or pen and then colour it in;
∗ make a design using pressed leaves;
∗ draw with a pencil onto foil to imprint a design;
∗ cut out shapes from gummed paper for an abstract design;
∗ use doilies or lace for an attractive edging.

Let the children choose a technique and the appropriate materials for making their card. When the cover is finished ask them to decide what message to write inside and scribe it for them.

Questions to ask

When do you send and receive cards? Why do people send cards? What sort of pictures were on the front of cards you have had? Which sort of card would you like to make? What colours will you use? Which materials do you think you will need? What are you going to write inside your card?

For younger children

Choose one technique, say the gummed paper abstract design, and let children make their own designs.

For older children

Provide cards and pressed flowers, which they can carefully glue in various designs onto their cards using fine brushes to apply just a tiny amount of white glue to the back of each flower.

Follow-up activities

∗ Make cards for a range of religious festivals, such as, Eid, Rosh Hashanah and Divali. Make sure that you decorate them appropriately, write inscriptions correctly and fold them in the correct way. Buy a selection of cards as examples if you are unsure.
∗ Set up a card workshop with materials, cards and examples for the children to work on independently.
∗ Make envelopes to fit some of the cards using envelopes opened out as templates.
∗ Make a large wall calendar chart and mark on it all the dates of the children's birthdays, festivals and other special days when cards are sent.

Dress a puppet

Learning outcome

To develop designing and making skills.

Group size
Two children.

What you need
Puppet heads made from papier mâché (about 10cm × 7cm × 7cm). Use the method for papier mâché described in 'Unbreakable plates' on page 43. Pieces of fabric for the puppet bodies. Scissors, sharp enough to cut the fabric (for adult use only), several sticks of white chalk, glue, large-eyed needles and thread, small pieces of felt, dressmaking pins.

Preparation
In an earlier session make the puppet heads with children using the papier mâché method. Paint them and outline the features. Make the faces represent a number of different characters, perhaps linking them to a familiar story. Cut out two glove puppet 'body' templates, which will have arms, a neck opening and a rectangular shape for the body. Cut up the pieces of fabric so that they are about 30cm × 45cm.

What to do
Tell the children that they are going to make a glove puppet. Explain that some of the tools that they are going to use are very sharp and they will have to be very careful. Let the children choose the fabric that they would like to use for their puppet's body. Show them how to fold it lengthways so that it is double thickness, with the right sides together. Help them to draw round the templates with the chalk, holding the fabric as still as possible. Pin the fabric together about 1cm inside the outline. Cut out the outline for the children, demonstrating how you are cutting along the chalk line.
Now help the children to thread up a needle and tie a large knot in the end. Show them how to sew the two sides of the material together. Large stitches won't matter, but encourage children to get the stitches as close together as they can. When the bodies are sewn up turn the fabric inside out. Fit the neck

of the puppet head into the opening and glue in place. Leave to dry. When fully dry, glue a pair of felt hands to either side of the 'arm' ends.

Questions to ask
Who is your puppet going to be? Which piece of fabric are you going to choose? Why do you like that fabric? How does it feel? Why is the chalk good for marking the fabric? How do you think your clothes are made?

For younger children
Make paper bag puppets, using plain paper bags and showing the children how to draw on faces with large felt-tipped pens.

For older children
Show the children how to make 'hair' for their puppets, by gluing on lengths of wool.

Follow-up activities
* Make a puppet theatre and act out familiar stories.
* Make wooden spoon puppets by drawing on felt-tipped faces and using them for simple play.
* Make animal stick puppets using the animal pictures on page 93. Colour the pictures, cut out and mount on card then stick onto clean lolly sticks.
* Draw faces on fingers and thumbs with a thin black felt-tipped pen and sing some finger rhymes together.

Links with home

Encourage parents to act out stories when they read to their child. Send home a letter with ideas for making simple stick, spoon and finger puppets. You might like to include a template for a design on the letter.

chapter seven

Drama and dance

In this chapter the children will learn new ways to move to stimuli such as music and story, develop skills of working with a partner and find out about ways to express their feelings through dance and drama.

Let's act it out

Learning outcome

To develop understanding of story structures and characterisation.

Group size

Whole group.

What you need

A large open space. A flip chart and black marker pen, a book containing the story you are going to use (choose one that the children are very familiar with and which has a good structure – fairy tales and folk stories are suitable, such as 'The Three Bears').

Preparation

Settle the children in your chosen area. Have the flip chart and pen next to you.

What to do

Read the story to the children and ask them to listen carefully. When you have finished ask them if they can remember what happened. Make a note on the chart of the main points that they suggest. Use the pictures from the book to help them. Draw the children's attention to the way the story has a beginning, middle and end, talk about the characters in the story and the action that takes place.

Look with the children at the notes you have made on the flip chart and try to sort these into scenes. For example,

Goldilocks eats the bowls of porridge, first Daddy Bear's, then Mummy Bear's and then Baby Bear's. This can form one scene. Ask some children to act out this scene as you tell that part of the story again. Decide on the next scene with the children and choose another group of children to act it out.

Questions to ask

Do you know this story? What happened in the story? What happened first? What happened next? What did the bears say? What happened at the end? Who were the characters in the story? How many people would we need to act out the story?

For younger children

Read the story through and then let the children tell you one thing that they remember about it. Perhaps their favourite bit?

For older children

Choose a story with a slightly more complex plot and more characters, so there is more interaction and more to recall.

Follow-up activities

∗ Make simple masks or props for the characters, such as bear masks and a wig for Goldilocks.
∗ Paint pictures of each of the scenes and mount these as a frieze.
∗ Make little books retelling the story with a scene on each page.

Links with home

Invite parents in to watch a simple performance of the story, using the props that the children have made.

Guess the rhyme

To retell rhymes through the medium of mime.

Group size
Whole group.

What you need
A book of rhymes, a flip chart and black marker pen.

Preparation
Allocate a clear space, such as a carpet area with some extra floor space. Sit in front of the children with the flip chart and pen beside you.

What to do
Sing five or six rhymes together and look at the pictures in the book that accompany the rhymes. As you sing each one write down the title, for example, 'Little Boy Blue'. After you have sung each rhyme talk for a few minutes about what happens in each of them.

Mime one of the rhymes clearly for the children, so that they can guess which one it is. Then ask one of the children to have a try. Encourage the child to whisper which rhyme they are going to mime (so that you can help them if necessary) and let them have a go at miming the rhyme while the other children try to guess. Repeat the process with other children having a turn. Try to choose rhymes with only one character in, such as 'Humpty Dumpty', 'Rock-a-bye baby', 'Ride a cock-horse' or 'Little Bo-peep' which include actions which can be mimed.

Questions to ask
Can you guess what I'm doing? Do you know which rhyme this is? Which rhyme have you chosen to mime? Which bit are you miming now?

For younger children
Let them sing and mime the rhyme at the same time.

For older children
Let them choose a rhyme of their own to mime which is not one you have written on the list.

Follow-up activities
✳ Make a chart listing all the nursery rhymes which the children know.
✳ Let children vote on their favourite rhyme.
✳ Paint pictures of the rhymes that have been mimed.
✳ Make some nursery rhyme character figures using pipe-cleaners for the bodies. Wind wool round the pipe-cleaners and make some simple felt clothes.

Links with home

Ask parents to play miming games with their child. Suggest that they mime simple everyday activities such as drinking a cup of tea, boiling a kettle or reading a newspaper for their child to guess.

Puppet fun

To explore ideas and feelings through using puppets.

Group size

Two to three children.

What you need

A puppet theatre (this can be made simply from a cardboard box with the front and back cut away). Puppets made by the children (see 'Dress a puppet' on page 52).

Preparation

Set up the theatre in a quiet corner, if it is small set it up on a table. If possible screen the area a little so that children are not distracted.

Questions to ask

Hello, who are you pretending to be today? How are you feeling? Why do you feel angry/fed up/excited? Can you tell me all about it? How do you feel about it now?

For younger children

Let younger children just explore their ideas as they play freely. Observe carefully to see what sort of stories they are acting out. Listen out for children who seem to be expressing worries during their play. You may need to have a sensitive discussion and provide support at a later date.

What to do

Show the children the puppet theatre and the puppets and explain that you are all going to have fun making up stories about the puppets. The important thing is to encourage the children to improvise the drama, so that they play out their ideas and emotions. Most children respond well to puppets and will readily begin to take on characters.

To help those children who are either shy or uncertain try suggesting a scenario, such as: 'This is Alice. She's really fed up today and doesn't want to go to school. Her Mum is getting cross. Make the puppets tell me what Alice is going to do'. It also helps the children to respond if you join in the play by taking on a puppet yourself. Try to create opportunities for the children to articulate some of the feelings they are keeping hidden.

For older children

Give the children character roles to play out, such as from television programmes which you know they watch regularly and are familiar with.

Follow-up activities

∗ As starting points, suggest the children imagine they are angry, excited, bored, tired or scared and that their puppets feel that way.
∗ Use these emotions as starting points for movement sessions.
∗ Suggest that the children do 'mood' paintings, choosing colours to match the feelings of anger, joy or sadness.
∗ Make a list with children of all the things that make them happy/sad/cross.

Links with home

Ask parents to tell you what their child likes doing best/least at home and what they really look forward to.

Tell-a-story figures

Learning outcome

To develop imagination through stories and imaginative play.

Group size

Two to three children.

What you need

A storyboard – this can be magnetic or a large sheet of cardboard covered with felt or other fabric. The story 'The Three Little Pigs'. Pictures of the three houses in 'The Three Little Pigs', pictures of trees and bushes, pictures of the story figures (use photocopiable page 94) mounted on card and backed with either magnetic tape or Velcro depending on the type of storyboard used.

Preparation

Make sure that children are familiar with the materials by allowing them to use them freely first. Set aside a small area of the room and screen it in some way (a three-sided clothes horse covered in material makes a good foldaway screen – these can often be found in jumble sales).

What to do

Read the story to the children. Talk about the story with the children, show them the characters and recap the main events of the story.

Put up the storyboard and give the children two or three characters each. Ask them to tell you the story using the figures. The children put their figures onto the board as needed and move them around while they tell the story. Sit back and listen, giving them support if they need it.

Questions to ask

Allow children to work through the story in their own way, if possible saving questions until the end. However should children need them, useful prompters can be: How does the story begin? What happened next? What happens at the end? Can you remember what he/she said? At the end ask: Did you enjoy that? Which bit of the story did you like best? Which was your favourite character?

For younger children

Set up the corner so that children can work on their own making up their own stories using the figures.

For older children

Let the children record their stories by switching on the tape recorder as they are retelling the story. Make up a set of cards of the story and ask the children to arrange them in sequence.

Follow-up activities

* Make sequence cards.
* Make additional figures to vary/extend the story.
* Make a theatre from a cereal box and stick puppets.
* Act out the story.

Links with home

Ask parents to read the story at home. Give them a copy of photocopiable page 94 to make the figures at home.

My journey to nursery

Learning outcome

To explore ideas by acting out a familiar journey.

Group size

Eight to ten children.

What you need

A space for the action away from other activities. Paper and a pen. A large sheet of paper and felt-tipped pen. A large map of the area around your school.

Preparation

Make sure that you have a clear area for the children to move about freely in. Keep the paper and pen with you to record any observations which may be useful later (for records or planning purposes). With the children, mark on the map where they live, the school and some of the main features of the area.

What to do

Seat the children comfortably together around you and discuss the ways in which they come to the group. Find out who comes by car, who walks and who comes by bus. Ask them to think about the things that they pass on the way. Talk about landmarks, such as shops, houses, railways or woods which they might pass. Who do they come with? Try to get an idea of how long it takes. Do you come in a hurry or do you come slowly? Do you enjoy your journey?

Mark one or two of the children's routes on the map. Take one of these as an example and ask the children to stand up and find a space. Explain that they are going to act out the imaginary journey – 'You're leaving your house now, shut the front door, walk down the steps...'. If children are enjoying the activity, try another child's journey which is slightly different. After you have tried a couple of journeys let the children freely recall and act out their own routes.

Sit down together at the end of the session and ask the children to think about their journey again. Did they forget anything? Is there anything they want to tell everyone about their journey? This reflection time is an important aspect of all drama sessions.

Questions to ask

Who comes by train? Can you remember which way you come? Do you go past any trees or a pillar box? Is it very busy? Can you remember anything else you do?

For younger children

Make the session shorter. Take an imaginary example and act this out. Discuss some of the children's experiences afterwards.

For older children

Let children work on their own routes in more detail. Suggest that they vary the mood – coming to nursery excited/ not wanting to come.

Follow-up activities

* Plot the rest of the children's routes on the map.
* Take the children for a walk around the area, looking at landmarks and features which can later be put on the map.
* Take photographs of some of these features and use the photographs as the basis of close observational drawings.
* Make a base board for small world play showing the local area (see 'Bases for play' on page 69).

Links with home

Ask parents if they can tell you how long their journey to nursery takes each day. Make a chart showing times for each child. Find out who has the longest/ shortest journey.

Ring-o-ring o' roses

Learning outcome

To develop enjoyment of circle dances.

Group size

Whole group.

What you need

A large, clear space where children can move freely. One or two adults as helpers. The song, 'Ring-o-ring-o-roses'.

Preparation

Clear the area you are going to use. Explain your plans to helpers.

Questions to ask

What shape have we made? Who are you next to? Can you change to stand next to two other children? Show me which way is left/right.

For younger children

Make circle games fun and encourage all the children to join in. Play a game each day, setting up the expectation of a regular, short and enjoyable activity.

What to do

Ask the children to make a ring and hold hands. Sing the song of 'Ring-o-ring-o-roses' with the actions. Make a new circle with everyone holding hands with a different person. Sing the song again. Ask the children if they know the name of the pattern they are standing in (circle, ring, round). With hands joined together circle round to the right taking six steps. Then circle to the left taking six steps. Do the same again both ways going a little faster, skipping slightly. Step into the middle taking three steps, and out again, taking three steps. Encourage the children to enjoy the feeling of moving together and sometimes going the wrong way! End the session by doing another circle dance, such as 'Here we go Looby Lou'.

For older children

Add one or two variations to your circle movements, such as going into the middle and clapping, and out again and clapping.

Follow-up activities

* Play a variety of circle games, such as 'Hokey Cokey', 'Here we go round the mulberry bush' and 'The farmer's in his den'.
* Let children paint pictures of the 'circle dance'.
* Talk about circles, use equipment and shape games with circles in, letting children handle and draw circle shapes.
* Make cut out figures in a row and join them together in a circle (by folding paper, drawing on one figure and cutting out so that the hands are joined).

Links with home

Encourage parents to draw their child's attention to circle shapes in the home – such as cups, plates and so on.

Take your partners

Learning outcome

To gain experience of dance patterns and to work with a partner.

Group size

Six children.

What you need

A clear space to work in, cassette recorder and cassettes.

Preparation

Find a piece of traditional folk or country dance music and select a short excerpt. Make yourself familiar with the rhythm of the piece.

What to do

Invite the children to find a partner and hold their hand. Ask the three pairs to stand in a line facing you. Tell the children to take six steps forward. Then six steps backwards. Practise a few times. Then ask the pairs to find a space. Holding one of their partner's hands let them skip freely around the space. Repeat with the music.

Turn the music off so that the children can concentrate on a new movement. Facing their partners and holding both their partners hands they should step forwards for six steps and backwards for six. Still facing their partner ask them to clap their partner's hands twice (their own if too difficult). Practise a few times.

Conclude the session by putting the music on again and letting the children dance freely with their partner for a few minutes.

Questions to ask

Can you find a partner? Can you make a line facing me? Which way is forward/backward? How do you know you are in a space? Are you going to skip quickly or slowly? What do you find hard/easy about this dance?

For younger children

Let children become familiar with folk dance rhythms by playing short pieces from the tape and letting the children dance freely.

For older children

Build up a sequence of the actions you have practised and repeat them, so that the children learn a dance pattern.

Follow-up activities

* Let children paint pictures of themselves and a partner. Mount these pairs in spaces on a large sheet of paper. Draw arrows to indicate some pairs going forward, some backwards and some sideways.
* Get some play figures and ask the children to put them into pairs. Suggest they move the figures, forward for two, back for two in a pretend dance.
* Play picture card games which involve finding pairs.

Links with home

Ask parents to play some simple partner games with their child, such as clapping or mirror games where they have to copy an action simultaneously.

A kite on a windy day

Learning outcome

To develop awareness of the weather and seasonal changes through dance.

Group size

Whole group.

What you need

The story 'The new kite', on page 83. A large, clear space for dancing.

Preparation

Clear the area and have the story ready to read, or memorise it in advance.

What to do

Ask the children to find a space. Let them warm up by moving their arms and then legs, shaking them vigorously and slowly. Suggest they move around the room stretching up and then swooping down lower, moving their arms and bending their backs. Then ask them to stand still in their space.

Explain that you are going to tell them a story and that you want them to do the movements as you go along. Show them what you mean by demonstrating how a tree might move when blown by a high wind. Begin the story and let children interpret each section. Encourage them to express their ideas in their own way. Make suggestions to remind them when to move slowly or fast and to encourage them to make full use of the space.

Questions to ask

Describe how you think the trees move in the wind. How does a kite go when it is flying high? Is it going fast? How do you think a kite goes when it is coming down? Is it going slowly? Is it falling? What happens to people's hats or hair on a windy day? What happens to the washing? How does it feel when you are walking on a windy day? Does the wind sometimes push you? Do you like windy days?

For younger children

Tell the story in advance and talk to them about it before starting the activity.

For older children

Let the children talk about some of their own windy day experiences and add these ideas to the story.

Follow-up activities

* Set up a windsock in the outside area to look at the force of the wind.
* Find a picture of a weather vane and talk about the way it is blown in different directions. Mention the terms North, South, East and West.
* Make some kites and test them out.
* Talk about kite festivals in China and other Eastern countries.
* Make a list of words which describe a kite flying – swooping, soaring and so on.
* Make a display of kites and books about them.

Links with home

Ask parents if they can bring in any examples of kites for your display. Ask them if they have any memories of flying kites which they could talk to their child about.

Animal antics

Learning outcome

To explore the ways that animals move and behave through dance.

Group size

Whole group.

What you need

A large, clear space.

Preparation

Think about the characteristics of several animals and prepare some ideas about the movements that you will ask the children to try and make. Clear the area ready.

What to do

Ask the children to move around the room, skipping and walking, to warm them up. Remind the children about safety and keeping a space around them.

Explain that you are going to describe lots of animals and you would like them to pretend to move around like those animals without making a sound. Take the children to an imaginary place where lots of animals live, children can slither like snakes, scratch like monkeys, stretch up their necks like giraffes and move stealthily like pumas stalking their prey. Choose a good range of animals with different sorts of movements, which will encourage the children to use different parts of the body. Use lots of descriptive vocabulary as you describe the animals' actions, such as hungrily, heavily, proudly and lazily. This will help to inspire the children's imagination.

Questions to ask

How do you think a snake moves? Does it move very quickly/slowly? Does it change direction or sometimes move suddenly? When do you think it would do that? Can you show me how your snake moves? Which part of the body are you going to use? Repeat with other animals.

For younger children

Talk beforehand about how animals move and concentrate on two or three types of contrasting movement.

For older children

Use more sophisticated vocabulary with older children and encourage them to put as much detail as they can into each different type of animal movement.

Follow-up activities

∗ Set up a zoo or a farm with small world play resources and let the children sort the animals by type. Try to have a few of each kind.
∗ Draw pictures of zoo animals, letting the children freely explore their emotional responses to the animals – for example they may want to paint their lion red because they think it is dangerous.
∗ Set up a table display with books about animals. Mount posters, photographs and children's pictures around it.
∗ Make tails, ears and masks for imaginative role-play.

Links with home

Ask parents if their child has been to a zoo and find out a few details. Try to arrange an outing to a zoo when parents can come too.

A walk in the woods

Learning outcome

To develop emotional and creative responses through music and movement.

Group size

Whole class.

What you need

A made-up story divided into four main scenes featuring different events/ moods for the walk. Base the story on familiar experiences, ideally take the children for a walk in the woods beforehand. A large, clear space. A tape recorder and appropriate music.

Preparation

Get the area ready. Divide the story into four scenes with distinct emotions to show the children:

∗ Walking through the wood (happy).
∗ Seeing a squirrel (excited).
∗ Wanting a rest (sleepy).
∗ Hearing a woodpecker (scared).

Make a tape with a selection of short pieces, one for each scene. Set the tape ready.

What to do

Ask the children to find a space. Warm up by asking the children to move their arms and legs on the spot. Explain that you are going to tell them a story about them visiting a wood and that you want them to act out the different scenes as you play the music.

Work on a scene at the time, telling the children the story in simple terms and playing the corresponding piece of music. The four different scenes will allow the children to express a range of different emotions.

Questions to ask

How do you feel when the sun is shining? Imagine you found a beautiful flower in the woods. How would you feel? What does the music make you want to do? You hear a woodpecker pecking, how are you feeling now?

For younger children

Focus on just two contrasting scenes.

For older children

Encourage the children to talk about their own experiences and add these ideas to the story.

Follow-up activities

∗ Discuss which piece of music the children liked best and which scene they enjoyed the most.
∗ Encourage children's bodily awareness and agility by having short sessions for stretching, bending, curling, swaying and crouching.
∗ Let children draw or paint pictures of the different story scenes.
∗ Go for a walk in woods in your area, to give the children first hand experience for their movement session.

Links with home

Invite parents to join you on an outing to some local woods. Make a list of things that the children might see on the outing in advance for parents to discuss with their child beforehand.

chapter eight

Imaginative play

Imaginative play forms an important part of a child's creative development in the early years. In this chapter the children will be given the opportunity to take on different roles and to create a variety of things to stimulate their imagination and develop their creative skills.

Going on a picnic

Learning outcome

To develop imagination and ability to role-play a situation.

Group size
Six children.

What you need
Picnic cutlery and crockery, thermos flask, a tablecloth, a picnic basket/bag, serviettes, a rug or blanket, items of picnic food, (real or pretend). The story 'Taki's picnic' on page 84. A corner of the room for the activity.

Preparation
Collect all the items together and set up the imaginative play area ready for a picnic. If you have screens, ask the children to paint some scenes of woods, fields and parks to stick on them.

What to do
Talk to the children about picnics – what sort of things do they eat on a picnic? What things do they do?

Tell the children the story of 'Taki's picnic'. Then show them the items that you have collected for the picnic. Talk about the items in turn, discussing what they are made of, and what they are for.

Allow the children to use the objects (removing delicate items such as the thermos flask, any edible food and ensuring that there is nothing sharp) and suggest that they pretend that they are having a picnic. Leave the children to devise their own play. Enquire from time to time how things are going.

Questions to ask
What is a picnic? What is special about a picnic meal? Have you ever been on a picnic? What did you do? Where did you go? What did you eat? What sort of food and drinks do you think you could have on a picnic?

For younger children
Let them play with the picnic items first to become familiar with them before having a discussion.

For older children
Discuss some of the problems that might occur when you are eating outside such as wasps, flies, damp grass or sand.

Follow-up activities
* Take children on a picnic, prepare the food together before you go.
* Make a list of the most popular food to take on a picnic.
* Talk about picnics in other countries, such as Christmas dinner on the beach in Australia, and picnics from the past, such as the sorts of picnic hampers their grandparents might have used.
* Bring in teddy bears. Learn the rhyme 'Teddy bears' picnic'.

Links with home

Ask parents if they have any unwanted items which you could use in the picnic corner. Invite parents to your picnic to share in the fun.

Sunshine tours

Learning outcome

To role-play 'at the travel agents' and to learn about other countries.

Group size

Four to six children.

What you need

A good assortment of travel brochures showing many parts of the world. Posters of travel scenes/ different countries, giving positive images of a range of cultures. A large wall map of the world and a map of the British Isles. A telephone, till, mobile phone, paper, pens, pencils and a calculator, computer, screen and printer (real or pretend). A play area, preferably with screens, some lengths of fabric for display, tables to create a 'counter'.

Preparation

Set up the area as a travel agents, putting the screens out as walls and the tables as a counter. Have all your other items to hand.

What to do

Talk to the children about what a travel agents looks like and ask them to help you put up the posters and set out the other items. Discuss what people go to travel agents for and talk about the people who work there and the customers. Talk about what customers have to do in order to book a holiday and show them some role-play examples. Divide the children into customers and workers and let them take on their roles.

Questions to ask

What is a travel agents? What does it look like inside? What do you do in a travel agents? Encourage the children to tell you about any holidays they have been on. Ask them if they can remember helping to choose the holiday. What can you remember about your holiday?

For younger children

Show them how to play in the area, with an adult taking on a role to demonstrate the tasks that both customers and staff might do.

For older children

Invite them to paint their own holiday pictures to decorate the agency. Help them to think about some captions to write out for the walls of the travel agents.

Follow-up activities

* Find out some exchange rates and make a list of currency exchange rates to put on the wall.
* Make 'tickets', 'booking forms', 'credit cards' and 'money wallets'. Have a supply of home-made currency notes and some real or pretend coins in different currencies.
* Talk to the children about where they have been on holiday and mark the places on the maps.
* Make a display of holiday souvenirs and postcards asking children to bring in some items.

Links with home

Ask parents to bring in items for the display table and to collect a few items for the display when they go on holiday.

Fire station

Learning outcome

To learn about the fire service through imaginative play.

Group size

Four to six children.

What you need

Screens, tables and space to set up a fire station corner. Fire helmets and tunics (available from The Early Learning Centre), play equipment (such as sections of hose, first aid kit, walkie talkie), telephone, writing-pad and pencils, plastic cutlery and a tea set. Pictures and books about fire-fighters (make sure that images include both men and women and a range of cultures). A large wall map of the local area and Blu-Tack to mark places on the map.

Preparation

Set up the play area as a fire station, with a table for the phone and writing items. Provide a box or hooks for the clothes and equipment. Provide a small eating area with cutlery and a teaset. Put up pictures around the area and hang up some of the books by threading a large rubber band round the centre pages and hanging them on a hook pin. Put up the wall map and have the Blu-Tack next to it. If possible, set up a 'fire-engine' nearby (made from large bricks, boxes or a wheeled toy).

What to do

Talk to the children about the fire station. Discuss who is likely to be there and find out how much children understand about what fire-fighters do. Talk about what happens when a 999 call comes in and how the crew are told where the fire is and how serious it is. Show the children how the map is used to indicate where the fire is (use a small piece of Blu-Tack to mark the spot), and how the crew use the map to work out the quickest route to the fire. Discuss the uniforms and the equipment used.

Explain that you would like them to pretend that they are all working at the fire station. Allocate the children some roles and suggest a simple scenario, then let them improvise. As the play progresses let children change roles as they wish, but keep an eye open for anyone monopolising equipment or over-dominating play.

Questions to ask

Do you know what to do if there is a fire? Tell me how you would call for help. Do you know what happens when a fire-fighter gets a call? How do they know where the fire is? Why do they have helmets? Why are they made like this? What is breathing apparatus for? Why do they need hoses? What happens if someone is hurt in the fire?

For younger children

Read stories about fire-engines and fire-fighters first, then set up the fire-engine and let them play freely on that.

For older children

Show children how to dial 999 and explain how they ask for the fire brigade and how they give simple information about where they are. Let them pretend to do this on the toy telephone.

Follow-up activities

* Arrange a visit to a fire station to see how it operates. Take photographs of the engines, equipment and fire-fighters in uniform.
* Set up a road layout for small world play with model fire-engines and a fire station.
* Talk about the colours of fire and smoke and do some colour mixing to create the colours.
* Learn the rhyme 'London's burning'.

Links with home

Ask parents to talk to their child about safety in the home and what to do in an emergency.

Snip 'n' style

Learning outcome

To learn about hairdressing through imaginative play.

Group size
Four children.

What you need
Home corner sink unit, washing-up bowls as 'basins', plastic trays with curlers, combs, brushes, hair-clips, old shampoo bottles, plastic scissors and hair nets. A table and chairs, old magazines, photographs from magazines of different hairstyles, pretend hairdryers, hand mirrors and a larger wall mirror, old towels, a telephone, till, some writing-pads and pens, soft toys and dolls (as customers), a camera.

Preparation
Set up the hairdressing corner, screening it off if possible. Put out chairs in the drying area and the wash-basins by the wall mirror. Put the other items on a small table or trolley. If you have screens decorate these with photographs of hairstyles – try to provide an ethnic, gender and age mix. Set up a telephone, with pads and pens and a till.

What to do
Talk to the children about visiting the hairdresser. Do any of them ever go to one? What sorts of things happen? Discuss hair-cutting, washing, styling and drying. Emphasise the importance of cleanliness and that the combs, curlers and so on are to be used on the toys or in pretend fashion. Explain that at the hairdresser's all the things are sterilised after they have been used to stop any diseases spreading.

Talk through the sequence of washing, cutting, styling and drying hair and encourage the children to start role-playing a visit to the hairdresser's. Allocate roles and ensure that the children share the resources and swap roles regularly. Make time to join in with the role-play to provide new ideas and maintain the children's interest and enthusiasm. Take some photos of the corner and of the role-play to use later.

Questions to ask
Who has been to the hairdressers? What did you have done? Have you seen anyone else have their hair done? What are curlers used for? What does shampoo do? Why do you need a towel round your neck? What are brushes and combs for?

For younger children
Read stories about going to the hairdresser's and play in the hairdresser's with them, to show them how to use the items.

For older children
Invite them to draw a picture and write a sentence about the hairdresser's.

Follow-up activities
∗ Make a collection of old shampoo bottles and talk about what shampoos are made of.
∗ Cut out pictures from magazines showing hair-styles and make collage pictures. Include styles from all racial groups, men and women, old and young.
∗ Make a list of words to describe how hair feels, such as smooth, wiry, fine, soft and silky.

Links with home
Ask parents if they could take a photo of their child at the hairdresser's or having their hair washed at home. The photos can then be mounted in their books.

Nine to five

To learn about working in an office through role-play.

Group size
Four children.

What you need
An area to set up the office, screens, tables and chairs, one or two computers, telephones, calculators, mobile phones and fax (real or pretend). Writing paper of various types, envelopes, pads/notebooks, diaries and other assorted stationery, pens, pencils, rubbers, scissors, rulers and markers. Boxes, trays and baskets to keep items in, a pinboard, a clock and a calendar.

Preparation
Set up the office, screening off the area (screens can be made very simply by attaching curtaining to old, wooden clothes-horses). Set out the office equipment and stationery items and make sure that there is room for four children to work at 'desks'. Fix up the pinboard to one of the screens as a notice board. Put up the clock and calendar.

What to do
Ask the children if any of their parents work in an office. What sort of work do they think people do in an office? Talk to them about some of the things that people might do, such as answering the telephone, writing letters, using computers, sending faxes, having meetings, ordering new stationery and so on.

Discuss how the office might look and talk about the various pieces of equipment, make sure that the children know what each piece of equipment is used for. Talk to them about general office hours – when people start and finish and how they have lunch and tea breaks.

Let the children play out their own ideas using their imagination to construct their office scenario. Be on hand to help them to develop their ideas and to provide new suggestions to enhance their play.

Questions to ask
What is an office? What do people do in an office? What sort of things do they use? What would they do when people phone up? What would they use the computer for? Why might they need a notice board? Tell me about your game. Are you a receptionist? What is your job at the office?

For younger children
Make a scrap book with lots of pictures of people working in offices. Look at the pictures with the children and talk about them. This will help to give them ideas for their play in the pretend office.

For older children
Extend their ideas by discussing some other sorts of offices, for example police station offices, bank offices and a school office.

Follow-up activities
✻ Visit an office in the area. Your local school may be willing to show you how theirs is run.
✻ Make a 'photocopier' from large cartons and cardboard. Paint it grey and add a logo.
✻ Talk about the importance of time and date in the office. Make a list of the lunch hour times and tea break times. Change the date each day and show how all letters are dated.

Links with home
Ask parents if they have any spare photos that they could let their child have to make 'office photos' for the work desks.

Mary, Mary...

Learning outcome

To learn about planting and growing seeds and plants.

Group size

Four children.

What you need

A corner of the room to set up the plant nursery. Packets of seeds – flower, vegetable and herb. Plug plants or seedlings, a selection of flower bulbs, plastic plant pots of various sizes, plant labels, small garden tools, trowels, forks, watering-can, dibber, a large bag of potting compost (peat-free), plastic seed trays, old plastic table cloth, tables, old newspapers, dustpan and brush. A large deep tray to hold the compost and pots while working. A collection of seeds for imaginative play (rather than for serious planting).

Preparation

Set up the area so that there is space for children to plant seeds, pot up plants and take cuttings. Put the plastic tablecloth down to protect the floor from potting compost which is easily spilled. Put sheets of old newspaper on the tables so that children can do some 'potting up' and sowing on there. Put one table to the side. Explain to the children that they must not put any of the seeds or bulbs near their mouths and they should wash their hands after playing in the area. Ensure that the activity in this area is always supervised.

What to do

Talk to the children about where we buy seeds and plants and how they are grown on a large scale. Tell them how people come to buy them from plant nurseries and that you are setting up a pretend nursery.

Talk about how seeds grow and show the children how to plant some. Put some potting compost into a seed tray and press down the compost lightly. Carefully open the seed packet and show children how to scatter the seeds over the surface.

Then cover with a very thin layer of potting compost. (Sieve this over the top using the hole in an empty flower pot as a sieve.) Show them how to handle the compost and to sweep up any spillages. Show children how to pot up the plug plants/seedlings and how to plant bulbs. Then let the children have a go at sowing and planting, then label the trays and pots carefully. Put on a side table nearby and explain that these are not to be disturbed. The other items can be left for children to use in imaginative play. Put out some of the seeds you are using for imaginative play, keeping back some for future sessions and for each new group of children using the area.

Questions to ask

What do you know about plant nurseries? What is a seed? How does it grow? Describe some of the seeds that you can see. How long do you think the seeds will take to grow? Do all the seeds take the same amount of time? How should we look after the plants?

For younger children

Sing songs and rhymes about growing and sowing, such as 'Mary, Mary, quite contrary' (Traditional) and 'Oats and beans and barley grow' in *This Little Puffin* compiled by Elizabeth Matterson (Puffin).

For older children

Do some experiments depriving some of the seeds of light and/or water and record what happens.

Follow-up activities

∗ Make plants and flowers, from sugar paper or thin card which can be fixed into pots with Plasticine and then 'sold' in the plant nursery. Make price labels for them.
∗ Do some close observational drawings or paintings of flowers, pot plants, or vegetables.

Links with home

Ask parents with gardens if they will plant out some of the vegetable seeds and keep you informed of progress.

Bases for play

To create a base board for use in imaginative play.

Group size
Two to three children.

What you need
A1 piece of strong card or hardboard, a large black felt-tipped pen, a thick pencil, papier mâché pulp made from torn-up newspaper pieces and a fairly thin solution of wallpaper paste (without fungicide). Paints and varnish, old newspapers, small pieces of card, glue, small pieces of sponge. Photocopiable page 95, lollipop sticks and colouring materials.

Preparation
Clear an area of floor or a large table to work on. Cover the area with newspaper. Keep the papier mâché, paints and varnish to one side until you are ready to use them. Make a copy of photocopiable page 95 for each group.

What to do
Decide with the children on the sort of base you wish to make. Ideas include – a road layout, a plan of your local area, a plan of your grounds, a park, farm, zoo, swimming pool, countryside or terrain for prehistoric animals.

When you have decided, help the children to mark out the base board with streets, hills, rivers and other features. Encourage the children to work together sharing their ideas. Suggest that they use pencil when they are working out ideas and then later ink in the final layout with felt-tipped pen. Hills and other raised areas can be created by sticking on papier mâché pulp and smoothing over to the desired shape.

Leave to dry out thoroughly (about a week) and once this is dry, the roads, rivers and fields can be painted on. The whole board can be varnished later. Trees and bushes, made from painted pieces of sponge and card can be stuck on, as can any buildings which are needed. Ask the children to colour in and cut out the signs. Stick them onto card and add lollipop sticks (or similar). Once complete use for play.

Questions to ask
What sort of layout do we want? What is it going to be for? Will you want it to be flat/have hills? What things would you like to include on it? Can you draw a road on the board? Can you make it wide enough for the cars? How do you think we can make a hill?

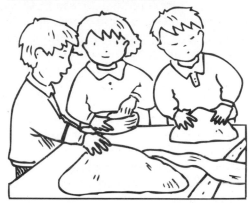

For younger children
Make a simple road layout, with fairly wide straight roads, a crossroads and zebra crossing. Use this to discuss road safety.

For older children
Ask the children to draw a simple plan of their layout before they start.

Follow-up activities
* Make a seaside layout with beach, harbour and sea and use with small boats.

* Make small buildings from reclaimed materials to use with the layouts.

* Show how plans and maps are made by photographing bricks or LEGO from above, photocopying the photograph and then tracing over it to provide the flat, two-dimensional image.

* Make traffic signs and notices, such as 'This way to the Zoo', 'Exit' and 'Caravan Park' to increase play potential.

* Build up a whole town or village scene by making a number of baseboards.

Kitchen furniture

Learning outcome

To design and make resources for use in imaginative play.

Group size

Four children.

What you need

Large cartons or medium-sized packing cases (such as a box used for containing a washing machine/other electrical appliances). Scissors, thick felt-tipped pens, a large dinner plate or small tray about 25cm diameter, masking tape, paints and thick brushes, a small piece of rope about 12cm thick.

Preparation

Make sure that you have a clear floor space to work in. Put down newspaper over the floor area and then place the carton/case on top. Put the scissors, plate, pens and tape near by. Mix up four containers of white paint to a fairly thick consistency and put a brush in each.

What to do

Talk to the children about what a washing machine looks like. Discuss the shape of the door and the way it opens. Seal up the ends of the carton with the masking tape. Then arrange it so that one of the smooth sides is facing you. Show the children how to draw round the dinner plate to make a large circle. Using the scissors cut round the circle for the children except for a 12cm strip on the middle of the left hand side. Carefully open the 'door' outwards bending back along this strip to create the 'hinge'. Make two holes in the opposite side of the door about 6cms apart and push the piece of rope through both holes from the outside. Knot both ends firmly on the inside – this forms the 'handle'. Invite the children to paint the case white and once dry, to draw on the control knobs and any brand names with a felt-tipped pen. Make other appliances in the same way and use for role-play.

Questions to ask

What shape is a washing machine? What size/colour are washing machines? Where is the door? What shape is the door? How do you think we can make a door that opens? How do you think we can fix on the handle?

For younger children

Involve them in painting just a small area of the carton.

For older children

Make four washing machines and two dryers and set up a launderette. Encourage the children to take on different roles and to play in their created setting.

Follow-up activities

∗ Make a range of kitchen appliances – a cooker, dryer, dishwasher, fridge, freezer and microwave. These can be used to make the basis of a café kitchen.

∗ Make a scrap book of electrical goods. Talk about their shape, size and the materials they are made from.

Links with home

Ask the children to have a look around their homes to see if there are any other items which they would like to make models of for imaginative play.

Take a hat and a bag...

Learning outcome

To develop imagination by using clothes and props.

Group size
Whole group.

What you need
A collection of bags, different scarves, different hats, shawls, lengths of fabric, old net curtains, old shirts, aprons, tea towels, dusters, dishcloths, a mop, plastic kitchen brush, notebooks and pencils, costume jewellery, old watches and suitcases, a collection of shoes, one or two newspapers and some comics, a thick black felt-tipped pen.

Preparation
Visit jumble sales and car boot sales to set up your collections. Wash the items carefully before the children use them. Include items from a range of cultures. Sort out some boxes for storage. Put all the items together, unsorted in a large box. Sit in a circle with the children on the carpet. Put the box by your side.

What to do
Bring some of the items out of the box and ask children what they are. Talk about who might use/wear the item. Let each child take an item out of the box and tell the group about it. If they want to, they can put the item on or hold it for a while. When everyone has had a turn and all the items have been looked at, set out the storage containers in the middle of the circle. Label these with the felt-tipped pen – shoes, hats, bags and so on. Then in turn ask each child to put their item into the appropriate box. Put these boxes into the imaginative play corner for free play.

Questions to ask
What is this? Who do you think might wear it? Who would use this? What would they do with it? If someone was wearing this where do you think they might be going? When would you wear a hat/shoes like this? What sort of things would you put in here?

For younger children
Limit the number of items you look at.

For older children
Start off a story 'Once upon a time there was a bag...' and ask them to carry on, telling you what comes next.

Follow-up activities
∗ Use some of the items for close observational drawings.
∗ Cut out pictures of hats, bags and shoes from magazines and make collage pictures.
∗ Ask children which is their favourite prop and photograph them wearing/using it. Mount the photo in their record book and write a sentence underneath.

Links with home

Ask parents to bring in old hats, bags and other accessories to build up your collections. Make a list of things that you need to give to them once a term.

What could this be?

Learning outcome

To use everyday objects imaginatively.

Group size

Eight children.

What you need

Some everyday items such as a magazine, a mug, some tickets, a letter and a key.

Preparation

Put the items together on a tray. Sit in a circle with the children and put the tray in the middle.

What to do

Pass the tray around the circle and let the children look at the items. Ask them to tell you about each thing. Then put all the items back in the middle.

Explain that you are going to play a game with the things, pretending that you found them and then guessing who they belong to and how they got there. Suggest a few ideas to start them off, such as, 'This is a letter from my grandmother, I think she must have dropped it when she was taking me to nursery', or 'I think this mug has been left by the workman who was mending the sink'.

Now let the children try. Allow them to try and think of their own ideas, but be ready to give them some help if they need it.

Once the children are confident with the game divide them into pairs and let them play the game together. After a few minutes gather the children in a group to share ideas.

Questions to ask

What can you see? What is this called? What is it for? What might you do with that? Who might use this? Imagine that you found all these items together. What do you think has been going on? Can you make up a story using these things?

For younger children

Leave the items out on a table and allow the children to play freely with them, seeing how they use them.

For older children

Write down some of the stories that the children make up and ask them to illustrate them.

Follow-up activities

∗ Vary the items used, changing the collection every week.

∗ Put out a large collection of items and ask the children to sort them into sets of things.

Links with home

Invite parents in to see some of the imaginative play that is going on and explain how the children are learning. Discuss some of the ways they can promote imaginative play at home.

Name _____

Child records

Creative Development		Assessment and comments	
Skills and concepts	Baseline/1st assessment Date	2nd assessment Date	End of year assessment Date
MUSIC			
Listens to: * sounds; * songs and rhymes; * musical instruments; * recorded music.			
Responds imaginatively to: * musical sounds; * movement sessions; * recorded music; * songs and rhymes.			
Shows awareness of: * high and low sounds; * fast and slow; * loud and soft.			
Can: * use musical instruments to express and communicate feelings; * stop and start when directed; * play a simple tune.			
Can recognise: * one beat; * two beats; * simple rhythm pattern.			

Child records

Name _____

Creative Development		Assessment and comments	
Skills and concepts	**Baseline/1st assessment Date**	**2nd assessment Date**	**End of year assessment Date**
ART AND CRAFT			
Can use tools such as: * brushes; scissors; mark makers; clay tools; hammers and screwdrivers.			
Can use a range of materials to make two- and three-dimensional models and artwork, such as: * paper; fabric; boxes; glue; paint/crayons/ printing blocks; clay/ pastry/Plasticine; natural materials; sand; water etc. Shows an awareness of texture when using these materials.			
Uses paintings and models to explore ideas of: * colour/shape/space; * three-dimensional form; * texture.			
Can express ideas and communicate feelings imaginatively through: * painting/drawing/ modelling etc.			
Responds to: * stimulus when painting/drawing/ modelling; * the work of artists and crafts people.			

Name _____

Child records

Creative Development	Assessment and comments		
Skills and concepts	**Baseline/1st assessment Date**	**2nd assessment Date**	**End of year assessment Date**
DANCE AND DRAMA			
Responds to: * stories; * songs; * music; as a stimulus for dance.			
Can express ideas imaginatively and communicate feelings through: * dance; * movement; * drama.			
Shows awareness of: * musical time; * pace; * rhythms; * mood.			
Can join in: * movement sessions; * musical games; * story telling; * individual dance work; * dance work with a partner.			

Child records

Name _____

Creative Development		Assessment and comments	
Skills and concepts	Baseline/1st assessment Date	2nd assessment Date	End of year assessment Date
IMAGINATIVE PLAY			
Takes part in: ✳ role-play; ✳ small world play; ✳ songs and rhymes; ✳ puppet play.			
Expresses ideas from experience imaginatively when: ✳ dressing-up; ✳ acting out stories; ✳ singing.			
✳ Can take on a role and sustain role-play. Shows an awareness of a variety of roles.			
✳ Can interact well with others during imaginative play.			
✳ Can use puppets and props to communicate feelings.			

Pattern making

I can make a pattern
with a zig-zag-zig.   (draw zig-zag in air)
First I draw a zig-zag,
bold and big.   (repeat (zig-zag)

Then I put the dots in,
blue, red, blue.   (dot 3 dots)
I can make a pattern.
How about you?   (gesture out to listener)

I can make a pattern
with a line and a dot.   (demonstrate line and dot on key words)
First I draw a line.   (mime)
Then I draw a dot.   (mime)

Line, dot, line, dot,   (mime this sequence)
that's the way it goes.
Line, dot, line dot: (mime sequence again)
now my pattern shows.   (gesture to imaginary pattern)

Tony Mitton

Going on holiday

(chanting rhyme)

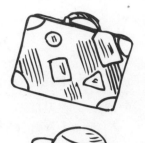

Germany, Austria, Switzerland too,
towering mountains, faraway view.

Bangladesh, Bosnia, Nigeria, Hong Kong,
we haven't seen our cousins for ... oh, so long!

Italy, Cyprus, Greece and Spain,
lots of sunshine, not much rain.

Take a jet to Florida, out in the sun.
Go and see an alligator ... ooh, what fun!

Shorts and sandals, sun-tan lotion,
going on a picnic, swimming in the ocean.

Train or car or boat or plane,
taking us on holiday and coming back again.

Tony Mitton

Painting

(poem for mimed actions)

Picking up a paintbrush,
trying not to dash.
Dipping it in water...
please don't splash!

Take a dab of yellow.
Take a dab of blue.
Mix them both together...
now there's green too!

Take a dab of yellow.
Take a dab of red.
Mix them both together...
there's orange instead!

It's time to clean your paintbrush.
Dip it in the pot.
Do you like painting?
Yes, I do... a lot!

Note: The mimed actions simply consist of picking up, dipping, mixing and leaning back to admire the results of one's imaginary work. The last line can be underpinned by a thumbs-up sign, if wished.

Tony Mitton

Can you hear?

The wind is a giant's breath,
I can hear him under my door.
He puffs and pants,
he moans and groans,
he whistles across my floor.

The rain is a million robins' feet,
tap-tapping on my door.
But the snow,
the snow falls silently
then the rain is heard no more.

Judith Nicholls

Animal chatter

A bee can buzz,
a dog can bark,
a cow can just say
'**Moo!**'
A sheep can bleat,
a blackbird sings
and a cuckoo says,
'**Cuckoo!**'

A bear can growl,
you can hear an owl,
a parrot squawks and
squawks!
A cat can mew,
a tiger roars,
but a tadpole
never talks!

Judith Nicholls

Give a hat, take a hat

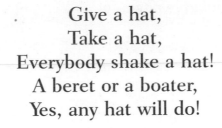

Give a hat,
Take a hat,
Everybody shake a hat!
A beret or a boater,
Yes, any hat will do!

Raise a hat,
Drop a hat,
Everybody swap a hat!
A flat cap or a fez
Will be very welcome too!

Hold a hat,
Hide a hat,
Has everybody tried a hat?
A top hat or a turban
Is just the hat for you!

Sue Cowling

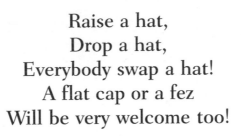

I am

(dialogue poem for shared voices)

'I am soft,'
says sponge cake.

'I am hard,'
says steel.

'I am rough,'
says tree bark.

'I am smooth,'
says apple peel.

'I am solid,'
says rock.

'I can bend,'
says grass.

'I am strong,'
says stone.

'I can smash,'
says glass.

Tony Mitton

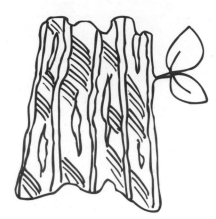

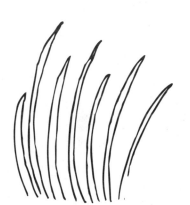

The new kite

Up on the hill, Simon unwound the string of his new kite.

'Now!' he shouted to his mum, and she threw the kite into the air.

Simon ran into the wind as fast as he could. When he felt the kite begin to rise, he stopped and turned round. The kite tugged his arms out straight in front of him. It danced and drifted pulling Simon first left, then right.

The wind grew stronger. He tried to pull his arms close to his body to rein in the kite, but it jerked them out straight again. He tried to dig his heels into the soft grass, but the kite tossed to and fro, and twisted him round.

Simon leant back into the wind, but the kite dragged him, first this way, then that, so that he couldn't stand still. The kite pulled him on, making him run. Up soared the kite. Up stretched Simon's arms. Higher still went the kite. Up onto his toes went Simon.

Then he could hold it no longer. The string slipped through his fingers. The kite floated off, out of reach. It danced and darted across the sky, as Simon stood and watched.

Suddenly the wind dropped. The kite twirled and tumbled. Down, down it fell, towards Simon's garden at the bottom of the hill. He chased after it and ran through the garden gate. A soft breeze began to blow. The kite swayed and slowed. The breeze rustled through the leaves of the fir tree outside Simon's bedroom window. As the kite floated gently down, the tree reached out its branches and caught it. And Simon sighed.

Jillian Harker

Taki's picnic

'Out you jump,' said Auntie Katerina, opening the car door. 'Let's find a place for this picnic.'

They set off, down the path through the woods. Mum took the food box. Auntie Katerina carried the blankets. Liandrou and Elena had the flasks. Alexander carried Taki, his toy dog. Alexander took Taki everywhere.

They soon came into a clearing. The sun dappled onto the big circle of grass.

'Taki thinks this is a good place,' said Alexander.

Everyone agreed. They spread out the blankets and unpacked the food. There were pittas and humus, baklava and fresh fruit, all piled high on bright plastic plates. There was orange juice and tea in coloured mugs. There was a huge leaf with twigs piled up in the middle of it.

'What on earth's that?' asked Aunt Katerina.

'Taki's picnic,' said Alexander. Everyone smiled and sat down to eat. It was silent except for the singing of birds.

'We could be the only people in the whole world,' said Elena. She lay back on the grass. It bent over her face and tickled her nose.

'Look!' called Liandrou. He pointed to a plant nestling among the grass. 'Tiny strawberries,' he said. 'Is it okay to eat them?'

'Wild strawberries,' said Mum. 'Yes, it's safe to try them.'

'Mmm,' said Liandrou. 'Best strawberries ever.'

'Taki thinks so too,' said Alexander, smearing one of the berries over the dog's nose. He wandered to the trees at the edge of the clearing.

'Let's play hide and seek,' said Elena.

'I'll play with Alexander,' said Aunt Katerina.

'I'll be *on it*,' called Mum. 'No wandering off too far. We don't want to lose anyone.' She counted to twenty.

'Got you, Liandrou,' she said, turning round. 'I can see your red T-shirt behind that bush.'

Before long she found Elena too, and then Alexander, who was squashed together with Auntie Katerina in some other bushes.

'That's everyone then.'

'No it's not,' replied Alexander. They all looked at him. 'You haven't found Taki.'

'Ah!' said Mum. 'Where exactly did you hide him, Alexander?'

'Behind a tree, of course,' smiled Alexander. They looked around the clearing. There were trees in every direction.

'It has a big trunk. I couldn't get my arms round,' Alexander added. Mum sighed. 'And the trunk felt rough,' said Alexander. Auntie Katerina rolled her eyes. 'And I put his plate of food by it,' smiled Alexander.

'Thank goodness!' they all said at once. In front of a large oak tree lay the huge leaf with the pile of twigs. Alexander ran over and picked up Taki.

'Taki really enjoyed this picnic,' he said.

'So did we!' laughed everyone else. And they followed Alexander as he swung Taki to and fro, all the way down the path, and back to the car.

Jillian Harker

Mixing colours

Johanne Levy

Learning in the Early Years
Creative Development

Rainbow song

Red for a ro - sy ap - ple,___ Or - ange for my

juice. Yel - low for the morn - ing sun - shine, Green for a ki - wi fruit.

Blue for the sky a - bove me, In - di - go at night. Vio - let like the

flo - wer, These col - ours make a rain - bow bright. Red, or - ange, yel - low, green,

1. Blue, in - di - go and vio - let.

2. Blue, in - di - go and vio - let.

Johanne Levy

Every colour under the sun

Calypso

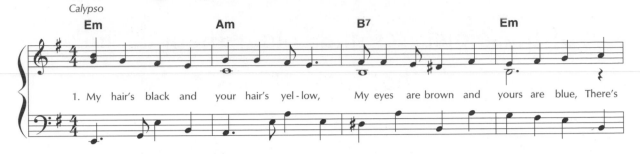

2. I'm quite old and you're much younger,
I'm very big and you're still small,
There's room on the earth for you and me,
There's plenty of room for all.
Chorus

3. I like snow and you like sunshine,
I like winter, you like spring,
There's plenty of both for you and me,
There's plenty of everything.
Chorus

Jan Holdstock

Listen carefully

Look at these pictures and colour them in. Talk about the sounds that these things make.

clock

dog

bell

cat

watch

whistle

drum

telephone

bird

Bang the drums

Which is the odd one out? Colour in the pictures.

Cut them out and put them in order of size.

Symmetry

Finish the pictures.

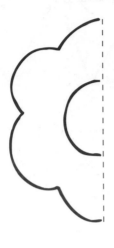

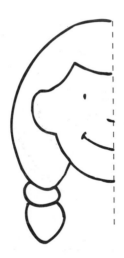

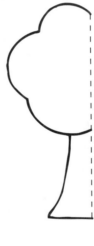

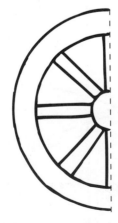

Blot painting (p38)

Junk modelling props

Cut out and use these shapes for your models.

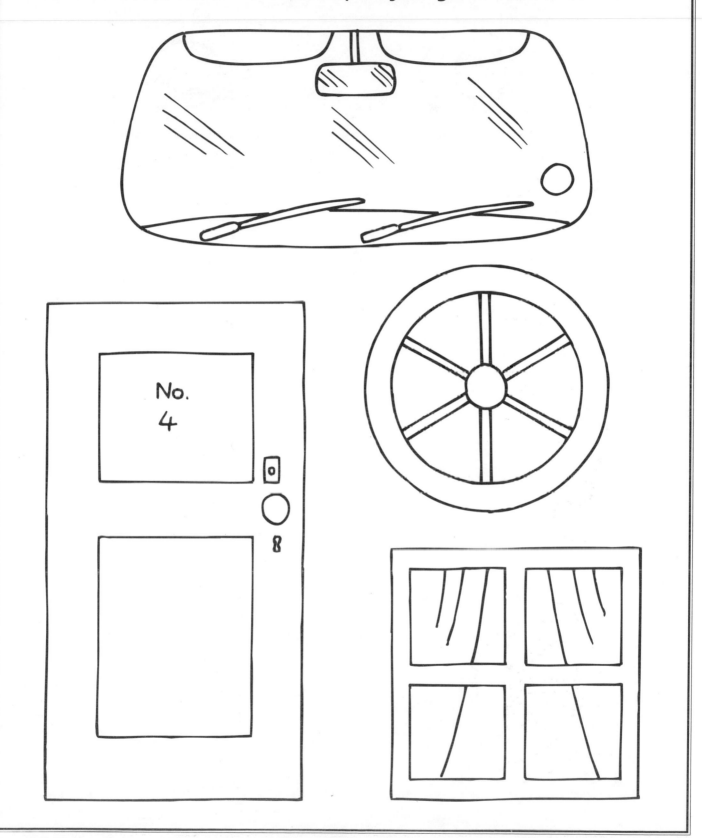

Fun with junk (p46)

Fun with hats

Match the hat to the person.

The mad hatter (p50)

Animal puppets

Colour in and cut out these animals to make into puppets.

Dress a puppet (p52)

Three little pigs

Colour in these animals to use with the story.

Tell-a-story figures (p56)

Signs to use

 Keep left

 Station

 To the Zoo

 cars only

 Greater City Railways High Town Station

 Southern Trees Park

 Excel Garage

 Shadows Shopping Centre

 one way system

Bases for play (p69)

Teacher reference books

'Music' *Eyewitness Guides Series* Neil Ardley (Dorling Kindersley)

'The Young Dancer' *Young Enthusiast Series* Darcey Bussell (Dorling Kindersley)

My Fancy Dress Book Cheryl Owen (Salamander Books)

Usborne Book of Puppets Cheryl Evans (Usborne Publishing)

'Van Gogh' *Famous Artist Series* (Franklin Watts Books)

Usborne Book of Easy Piano Tunes P Hawthorn and S Armstrong (Usborne Publishing)

Some Crafty Things To Do Karen Hale (Oxfam)

'Clay and Dough' *Learning through play series* Lynne Burgess (Scholastic)

A World of Display Judith Makoff and Linda Duncan (Belair Publications)

'Learning through play' *Bright Ideas for Early Years Series* Linda Mort and Janet Morris (Scholastic)

Helping Children to Draw and Paint in Early Childhood John Matthews (Hodder and Stoughton)

Music, Mind and Education Keith Swanwick (Routledge)

Creative Children, Imaginative Teaching Florence Beetlestone (Open University Press)

Rhymes, songs, tales and poems

Round and Round the Garden Ian Beck (OUP)

Usborne Nursery Rhyme Songbook Illustrated by Radhi Parekh (Usborne Publishing)

This Little Puffin... compiled by Elizabeth Matterson (Penguin)

Teddy Bears Picnic Mark Burgess (Harper Collins)

'Action Rhymes' *Kingfisher Nursery Library Series* selected by Sally Emerson and Pie Corbett (Kingfisher Books)

First Verses: Finger Rhymes ed. John Foster (OUP)

Orchard Book of Nursery Stories Sophie Windham (Orchard Books)

Kingfisher Nursery Collection Colin Maclean and Moira Maclean Kingfisher Books)

First Poems compiled by Julia Eccleshare (Orchard Books)

Owl and the Pussycat Edward Lear, illustrated by Louise Voce (Walker Books)

Puffin Book of Verse ed. Eleanor Graham (Penguin)

Books to use with children

Let's look at colours Nicola Tuxworth (Lorenz books)

Two can Toucan David McKee (Beaver Books)

The Mixed-up Chameleon Eric Carle (Penguin)

Activity books

Three Singing Pigs – Making Music with Traditional Stories Kaye Umansky (A & C Black)

'Paperplay' *You and Your Child Series* Jenny Tyler and Ray Gibson (Usborne Publishing)

Useful addresses

Write or telephone Scholastic for a catalogue of other early years teaching resources, which includes the series' *Learning Through Play* and *Themes For Early Years*:

Customer Services
Scholastic Ltd
Westfield Road
Southam
Leamington Spa
Warwickshire
CV33 0JH
Telephone: (01926) 813910

The Pre-school Learning Alliance (PLA) publishes a series of booklets called *Play Activities* on 'Gluing', 'Make-believe play', 'Sand and water', 'Clay and dough', 'Wood play' and 'Books and stories'.
They are obtainable from:
Pre-school Learning Alliance
Mail order house
45–49 Union Road
Croydon
CRO 2XU
Telephone: (0181) 684 9542